W9-CDA-642

ADVERTISING, POLITICS, AND AMERICAN CULTURE

ADVERTISING, POLITICS, AND AMERICAN CULTURE

FROM SALESMANSHIP TO THERAPY

PHILIP GOLD

PARAGON HOUSE PUBLISHERS
New York

Published in the United States by

Paragon House Publishers
90 Fifth Avenue
New York, New York 10011

Copyright 1987 by Philip Gold

All rights reserved. No part of this book
may be reproduced, in any form, without written permission
from the publisher, unless by a reviewer who wishes to quote
brief passages.

Library of Congress Cataloging-in-Publication Data

Gold, Philip, 1948–
    Advertising, Politics, and American culture.

    Includes index.
    1. Advertising—United States.   2. Advertising—
Social aspects—United States.   3. Advertising,
Political—United States.   4. Advocacy advertising—
United States.   I. Title.
HF5813.U6G58   1986   659.1'0973   86-30291
ISBN 0-913729-35-3

THIS ONE'S FOR ARLINE

CONTENTS

Part Four: **Res Publica**

PERMISSIONS AND ACKNOWLEDGMENTS

With thanks and gratitude:

At Georgetown University, Professors Dorothy Brown and Emmett Curran, for their teaching, guidance and care. Connie Holden, for the same and for listening and for occasional well-timed injections of reality. And Patricia Watkins, for unusual kinds of encouragement.

At Paragon House, Ken Stuart, Carroll Ann Brooks, Helen Driller and Charles Decker, for their patience and their skills.

And a special thanks to Irving Kristol, who knows why.

PREFACE

It is neither nice nor not nice. It is simply there as part of
the world we live in.

Leo Bogart
The Strategy of Advertising

The image, the commercial, reaches out to sell more than
a service or product; it sells a way of understanding.

Stuart and Elizabeth Ewen
Channels of Desire

The subject of this book is the world we share—that latticework of premises and expectations, meanings and bewilder-
ments, disappointments and ideals, compromises and surfeits
which bind us together beyond any unbinding. The approach
is via consideration of one aspect of that common world,
advertising: a product, a profession, an institution, and a system of discourse at once ubiquitous and trivial, inept and dom-
ineering, brilliant and mindless, creative and sterile, amusing
and detestable, familiar and bizarre. The theme is that advertising, *as a system of discourse,* is a luxury this civilization can no
longer afford.

At issue here is not advertising's purely economic function, which might best be described as legitimate and profli-
gate. (Of course, the same might be said of the Pentagon.) Nor
is the issue here that tired old debate over whether advertising
induces people to spend money they don't have on things they
don't need. (The same might be said of the Congress.) Nor is
the issue whether or not advertising inculcates and legitimizes
allegedly undesirable or immoral practices and values. (The

same might be said of the Supreme Court.) Nor is the issue whether advertising's putative "evils" can be eliminated by governmental regulation. They've tried, and if Washington bureaucracies were eligible for best-comedy awards, a string of 1970's Federal Trade Commission decisions would surely rank among the prime contenders. Rather, the issue under consideration here, to oversimplify a bit, is this:

What has advertising, as a system of discourse, done, and meant, to American civilization?

I came upon this question accidentally.

One bright autumnal day a few years ago, as the price of gas was accelerating past a dollar a gallon, inflation was generally ratcheting us all, the Iranian hostage crisis had become a fixture of national life and Jimmy Carter was busily and officiously lecturing the entire Republic on something called "malaise," I was driving my much-cherished yellow Volkswagen along Virginia's George Washington Parkway, scanning the architecture across the Potomac and paying marginal attention to the radio DJ's patois. He spun a song, then launched into the text of an ad for some behemoth American car; I no longer remember which one. He droned on through the model's and the dealer's reasons-why, then flexed his voice for the final pitch:

"Remember, riding out hard times in style is important to a guy like you."

Involuntarily, I said aloud, "This ad is . . . wrong."

Wrong?

I wondered what I meant by *wrong.*

The answer lies herein.

INTRODUCTION

It dominates the media, it has vast power in the shaping
of popular standards, and it is really one of the very limited groups of institutions which exercise social control.

David M. Potter
People of Plenty

Practically nobody likes it.

Stephen Fox
The Mirror Makers

What is it?

A moment ago I defined advertising as, at once, a product,
a profession, an institution, and a system of discourse. A product: the millions (billions? trillions?) of advertisements which,
in all their forms, suffuse what Kenneth Boulding has called
the "sociosphere," the artificial ecology of our lives. A profession: a hypercompetitive, albeit also surprisingly close-knit,
group of men and women who live and move and have their
being within a particular trade, in this case a business practiced, for the most part, in a few major cities by a few dozen
major agencies. An institution: a part of this culture, secure in
its place and multiplicity of roles, and not about to go away.
And, finally, a system of discourse that never existed before
and that represents the antithesis of rational discourse and
public dialogue as these have been known in Western
civilization.

Now, the idea that advertising constitutes such an unprecedented and potentially catastrophic phenomenon may not be
exactly self-evident. So, before exploring the notion further, it

might be well to approach the subject by concentrating on its more familiar aspects.

At the start of his venerable advertising textbook, Otto Kleppner suggested that "The urge to advertise seems to be part of human nature."[1] He had a point, albeit only a partial one. In essence, advertising is persuasive or manipulative (depending, I suppose, on one's point of view) communication, an activity at least as old as language itself. Behind every advertisement lies the desire to produce some effect, whether to motivate the consumer to purchase, the citizen to vote, or the human being to feel better (or less ill) disposed toward some idea, institution, issue, event, or cause. Almost invariably, the advertiser intends that the attitudes and actions he attempts to induce shall bring him benefit—almost invariably, because *circa* A.D. 1970, the Federal Trade Commission began ordering selected advertisers to undertake and pay for "corrective advertising" (a capitalist form of Marxist self-criticism, but more on that later).

Further, by definition, advertising is paid, self-interested, persuasive and/or manipulative communication. The advertiser or, more usually, his agency, purchases page space or air time and maintains—subject to certain minimal legal, aesthetic, and ethical constraints—editorial control over what fills that space or time. This differentiates advertising from other forms of publicity, such as press releases or "media events," in which the releasing or staging agency loses control over what ultimately appears. The advertiser also usually identifies himself somewhere in the ad: Exxon, National Rifle Association, Yuppies for a Nuclear-Free Pittsburgh, etc. Advertising individuals and organizations may not always be precisely who or what they claim to be, but some sort of identification is almost always part of the ad.

Advertising, then, is paid, self-interested, persuasive and/or manipulative communication emanating from a usually identifiable source. It is also mass communication. An advertisement is public, accessible to any and all who come into contact with it, or with the medium that carries it. This does not mean, however, that ads are aimed indiscriminately at the masses. Far from it. Most ads target particular audience or market segments. For example, while nearly all producers of branded goods seek to inculcate loyalty among consumers, many find it advantageous to concentrate on heavy users of their kind of product—groups that may be only a small percentage of the market numerically, but which nonetheless generate most of the sales. For example, a six-pack-a-night, two-fisted beer drinker obviously provides a more lucrative target than a temperance zealot or an occasional sipper. Thus, an ad that endears itself to the committed minority can afford to ignore, or even to alienate, an audience majority that has no special taste for or interest in the product. The folks at Miller or Anheuser-Busch may experience a certain regret that some non-drinkers or light imbibers don't appreciate their ads, but economically it matters not at all. (Of course, it may matter in other ways, but more on that later.) Similarly, Mondale-for-President advertisers never expected to have much impact on right-of-Reagan Republicans. Instead, they tried to reach the independent, the uncommitted, the wavering, and also the more tepidly faithful whose spirits might have needed stiffening as the campaign plodded toward disaster. Those who found Mondale's advertising inane, offensive, annoying, or fraudulent, usually just tuned it out.[2]

And it is precisely this "ignorable" quality of advertising which constitutes its distinctive feature as a system of discourse. As Michael Schudson has pointed out: "Advertisements ordinarily work their wonders, to the extent that they work at all, on an inattentive audience."[3] This is not necessarily the result of premeditated, intentional public hostility. Rather, it is due to the fact that every advertisement must compete with every other advertisement, not only for influence, but also for attention. Toothpaste may not compete directly with breakfast cereals in the marketplace, but their ads do in print and on the air. This competition is incessant and, from the audience's point of view, almost totally numbing. Thus, advertising must be designed not only to persuade and/or manipulate, but also to gain the attention of people who generally have neither the time nor the reason to be interested.

In fact, most advertising is simply never noticed by what Raymond A. Bauer once aptly and despairingly called "the obstinate audience."[4] This public resistance occasionally manifests itself in unusual ways:

> In 1953, the city engineers of Toledo, Ohio, raised a mild furor in advertising circles by releasing a chart of water consumption during evening hours, which showed great spurts of activity every half hour. This suggested that during the station break, when many commercials typically appear, a substantial part of the living room audience left for the kitchen or bathroom . . .[5]

(Of course, the more modern form of evasion tends toward what is known in the trade as "zapping"—changing channels by remote control whenever a commercial appears. But for those who have wondered why commercial sound tracks often seem a bit louder than the regular programming . . . *they know where you are.*)

In sum, then, advertising is paid, self-interested, persuasive and/or manipulative mass communication. It is also intrusive communication, almost inevitably part of something else, whether newspaper, magazine, or program. And even when it exists independently, in forms such as direct advertising (so-called "junk mail") and roadside billboards, it creates a number of waste disposal and aesthetic problems which often render it at least as disagreeable as program interruptions or seemingly endless stretches of commercial print. Thus, an advertisement must compete, not only with ads for similar and substitute products, as well as with every other ad swirling about in the environment, but also with the programming and reading matter whose very existence advertising usually makes possible—but whose message the recipient most often prefers.

(A small caveat here. Most people, according to newspaper lore, seem to prefer the ads to the news stories, perhaps because newspaper advertising brings the reader consistently good news, which cannot be said of the other departments. Also, sophisticated magazines such as *The New Yorker* often find their advertising at least as strong a purchaser/subscriber inducement as their other features.)

And, finally, advertising—indeed, mass-mediated communication in general—differs from direct, non-mediated communication in a vital way. Whereas in direct, non-mediated communication the sender of a message can gauge audience reaction in a number of ways (words, gestures, expressions, or lack thereof), the sender of a mass-mediated message must rely almost entirely on statistical feedback. Who and how many watched the show or read the magazine? Who and how many noticed the ad or remembered it or were influenced by it? Who actually bought the product or cast the vote? Over the decades, advertising has developed an extensive repertoire of techniques designed to measure audience responses, from "pre-testing" and simple post-appearance surveys to non-directed interviews and physiological reaction studies. But no matter what the form of individual response, it matters only in the aggregate. And, perhaps not surprisingly, all this research and technology has yet to demonstrate any firm, consistently replicable, predictively valid, general correlation between audience perception, recall, and emotional/aesthetic response and the creation of motivation to buy, vote, or believe.

Thematically, advertisements fall into four broad categories. The first, and by far the largest, encompasses product and service advertising, everything from the newspaper classified section (used banjo for sale: good sound, no strings attached), to transient retail notices (chicken breasts, 89¢/lb. thru Sat.), to the most sophisticated, long-range, expensive, multi-media campaigns for nationally marketed goods *(Coke Is It!)*. This type of consumer advertising, and its cousin, industrial advertising (for goods and services used in business and industry) includes the bulk of all advertising, both in quantity and in expenditure.

In second place comes institutional or image advertising: messages designed, not to sell anything in particular, but to foster a more favorable (or less unfavorable) attitude toward a particular institution. Oil companies and public utilities routinely spend a great deal of money on this type of advertising, both enterprises blessed with undeniably captive clienteles. AT&T, for decades prior to its breakup and the advent of cutthroat telecommunications competition, relied almost exclusively on institutional advertising, except for instrument and long-distance promotions. This kind of image advertising may indeed be aimed at the masses *qua* masses, although more often it targets an organization's special "publics," such as employees, stockholders, customers, creditors, etc., and real or potential adversaries such as the government, the media, and consumer groups.

Somewhat akin to image or institutional advertising is advocacy advertising: the use of paid messages to advance a point of view on some specific issue or other. This may range from matters which directly affect an organization's economic health or legal status (windfall profits taxes on oil, the ban on televised cigarette advertising) to long-term "aditorial" or "advertorial" campaigns by which corporations such as Mobil regularly purchase newspaper op-ed space to offer commentary on a wide variety of issues. When such advocacy advertising is undertaken by non-profit or "activist" groups to advance specific causes (Pro-Life, Pro-Choice, Pro-Contras, Pro-Star Wars, Pro-Whales), it is sometimes referred to as "consciousness advertising," a phrase that purports to distinguish it from mere corporate advocacies. Historically, the Advertising Council, a non-profit professional group, has produced or underwritten a large number of "public service" campaigns, perhaps the most famous being Smokey the Bear's ursine crusade against forest fires.[6]

The final category comprises electoral advertising. While the use of advertising in American politics goes back as far as American politics, it was not until 1952 that adman Rosser Reeves conceived that a presidential candidate might effectively be vended to the electorate by employing a format hitherto reserved for the merchandising of toothpaste, analgesics, cigarettes, and soap. General Eisenhower agreed, and a series of television spot commercials was prepared:

| Citizen: | "Mr. Eisenhower, what about the high cost of living?" |
| Eisenhower: | "My wife Mamie worries about the same thing. I tell her it's our job to change that on November 4th." |

Between takes, the General was heard to say: "To think that an old soldier should come to this."[7]

And thus the system: paid, self-interested, intrusive, persuasive and/or manipulative, statistically oriented, mass-mediated communication with a panoply of economic, political, cultural, social, and ethical uses—and also a system whose precise effects have never been, and perhaps never can be, determined in any final sense, and whose product is, by and large, ignored. All in all, a rather curious system, to be expected to help drive the Gross National Product ever higher, to elect men and women to offices of global power, and to determine the creeds, beliefs, aspirations, ambitions, desires, and ideals of hundreds of millions of human beings.

A curious system indeed.

PART ONE

THE SYSTEM DEFINED

THE AMERICAN AD

Whatever is common is despised. Advertisements are
now so numerous that they are very negligently perused,
and it is therefore become necessary to gain attention by
magnificence of promise, and by eloquence.
Samuel Johnson
The Art of Advertising (1759)

Love That Soap

Frederic Wakeman
The Hucksters (1946)

Advertisements graced the walls of Babylon. Millennia later,
Dr. Johnson could opine that "the trade of advertising is now
so near perfection that it is not easy to propose any improvement."[1] He may have had a point, at least insofar as the basic
repertoire of human wants and follies has remained relatively
stable since the first advertisement-expedited act of exchange
in some primordial economy. *Mutatis mutandis,* life still comes
down to the basics: food, clothing, shelter, the accoutrements
of status and companionship, and self-adornment of various
physical and psychological kinds. But for advertising to evolve
into what David M. Potter has called "the institution of abundance," and thence into something quite a bit more complex,
required the convergence of a novel set of circumstances: a
confluence that not only rearranged inherent priorities of
need, but also the constellations of meaning engendered by
those needs.[2] In the United States, this confluence occurred
gradually, throughout the latter part of the nineteenth century
and the first few decades of the twentieth.

Of paramount importance was the creation of an integrated national economy, itself the product of three new

forces: rapidly expanding population (especially in the cities), the economic unification of the country by the transcontinental railroads, and the rise of mass production. Along with the advent of extensive national commerce came new forms of selling, most notably the direct mail-order catalogue and the fixed-price, self-service retail store—an evolution in its way no less profound than changes in modes of production. As Daniel Boorstin has pointed out, the market gradually ceased to be a specific locale, an *agora*, and became instead a mass of (from the corporate point of view) anonymous individuals, related to each other (again, from the corporate point of view) only by their desire for or aversion to particular commodities.[3]

In short, the new national market was primarily statistical, and no longer personal. An individual might still consider the corner grocery or the downtown department store as the market for his or her limited transactions. Great national manufacturers, however, could not, and often found themselves perilously dependent on local middlemen and jobbers for the disposition of their wares. This condition, coupled with an almost total lack of reliable marketing data (outside of the information provided by orders, or the lack thereof), drove the captains of industry to seek a greater measure of control over sales. Means by which such control might be established included monopolization, the formation of trusts and cartels, and a wide variety of arrangements euphemistically known as gentlemen's agreements. Such methods could produce economically gratifying results, but occasionally gave rise to unpleasant legal problems and/or extralegal retaliatory acts by aggrieved competitors. A less effective, but also less questionable and hazardous technique involved pre-selling the merchandise. By opening communication with the ultimate consumer, a manufacturer might hope to increase, or at least stabilize, the level of aggregate demand for his products, and *en passant* minimize reliance on the promotional enthusiasms of local middlemen and jobbers. In short, somewhere around a century or so ago, American big business began to realize that a number of benefits might flow from subjecting the consumer to an introductory course in what later became known as brand loyalty.

The advertisement served as text.

Prior to the second half of the nineteenth century, the advertisement performed an essentially informative function—"the news of the store," in copywriter John E. Powers' apt phrase.[4] The hyperbolic pronouncements of P. T. Barnum and several legions of nostrum vendors notwithstanding, most ads merely announced the availability and commented on the special virtues of specific merchandise up for sale. Ads were news, usually embellished and more than occasionally fraudulent, but news nonetheless. Such notices, of local and temporary interest, and often exceedingly dull, were generally written and placed by retailers (who did their most effective selling face to face inside their stores). Toward the latter part of the nineteenth century, however, this began to change. Mass circulation newspapers and, more slowly, magazines began accepting more ads and more provocative ads. National manufacturers began to enter the field. The modern advertising agency was born.[5]

"The first advertising agent in the United States," relates trade historian James P. Wood, "went mad."[6] Originally, ad agents worked for newspapers, not advertisers, selling nothing more than blocks of page space and receiving commissions from the publication served, plus whatever they could garner by misrepresenting the rates to the advertiser and then pocketing the difference. Between 1841 and 1845, Volney B. Palmer broke this pattern, setting up his own offices in Philadelphia, New York, and Boston to handle a number of different papers on a competitive basis. For reasons probably connected with his enterprising life-style, he went violently insane and it was S. M. Pettengill, his understudy-turned-rival, who took the revolutionary step, not only of selling space, but of writing the ads themselves. In effect, this meant that the agent was becoming more the instrument of the advertiser than of the medium, a reversal institutionalized in 1875 when F. Wayland Ayer established the "open contract." Under this arrangement, Ayer (who named the agency he founded N. W. Ayer *and Son,* in order to acquire some instant longevity) charged a standard fee, billed the client directly, assumed responsibility for ad preparation, and even offered rudimentary marketing advice. According to dubious legend, Ayer even performed the first marketing survey, from which humble origin later arose the kindred arts of consumer and political polling.[7]

During this period, media themselves were becoming both more amenable to advertising and more easily utilized. George P. Rowell created *Rowell's American Newspaper Directory,* a publication providing the first reasonably accurate survey of newspaper circulations and practices. Cyrus H. K. Curtis developed a new genre of heavily commercialized magazines, such as *The Saturday Evening Post* and *The Ladies' Home Journal.* J. Walter Thompson, founder of the agency which still bears his name, helped to open the pages of higher quality magazines to advertising. Finally, Earnest Elmo Calkins, co-founder of Calkins & Holden, pioneered the integration of art and copy to produce a new style of "soft-sell" advertising appropriate for the more dignified media.

Thus, by the beginning of the twentieth century, the apparatus of modern advertising was substantially in place: mass market, mass media (minus, of course, the electronic media), and the "full-service" agency. The usefulness of the advertisement, concludes Otis Pease in his study of the profession's early years, had been "'sold' to the manufacturer as a competitive tool which was supposed to assure him a measure of control over his price, his merchandising policies, and his margin of profit."[8] And, on numerous occasions, advertising had provided far more than that "measure of control." By the early twentieth century, spectacular advertising-induced success stories for everything from soap to cereal to shoes to railroad travel had become a familiar part of American business lore and cultural heritage. Advertising had been proved capable of generating and sustaining success and, to a lesser degree, had also become respectable. And now, as the new century began, all the admen had to do in order to launch the classic age of modern advertising was to change their understanding of the nature of the ad, their calling, and the human race.

Albert D. Lasker was a tortured man. Though the transplanted Texan would dominate Chicago advertising (and much of the business as a whole) for nearly half a century, he spent the early part of his career in a torment of doubt. "More and more," writes his biographer, John Gunther, "Lasker became determined to find out what advertising really was." The matter became an obsession, a quest:

> He continued to be amply aware of the magic resounding effects it could have, but what, he asked himself, gave it those effects? . . . It was not primarily desire to get ahead that stimulated him, nor greed for money; it was a burning interest in a concept, an idea—it was curiosity. He implored his elders, "Teach me!" But no one knew more than he did, or could give him answers that satisfied him.[9]

The kairotic moment came in 1904 when, as the legend goes, Lasker was chatting with one of the founders of the Lord & Thomas agency (his employers) when:

> Following a polite knock, an office boy came in with a note and handed it to Thomas. Upon reading it, Thomas snorted and gave it to Lasker. The note said: "I am downstairs in the saloon, and I can tell you what advertising is. I know that you don't know. It will mean much to me to have you know what it is, and it will mean much to you. If you wish to know what advertising is, send the word 'yes' down by messenger." It was signed by a John E. Kennedy.[10]

Mr. Thomas, for his part, seemed unimpressed, but the desperate young Lasker wanted more. He sent down the proper word, and:

> From that time on, Lasker knew what advertising was. First Kennedy asked him what his own ideas were, and Lasker mentioned news. Kennedy said, "No. News is a technique of presen-

tation, but advertising is a very different thing. I can give it to you in three words." Lasker said, "I am hungry. What are those three words?"

Kennedy said, *"Salesmanship in print."*[11]

And thus was codified an essential change. The basic idea was, of course, hardly new. But to Lasker the maxim seemed possessed of a certain Pauline quality, and Lord & Thomas became the first major avowed practitioners of "Reason-Why" advertising—the philosophy that the consumer must be, not merely attracted and informed, but ardently pursued, persuaded, and cajoled. It may all seem obvious today, but how often it is that the obvious seems so only in retrospect.

Lasker hired Kennedy on the spot. He stayed with Lord & Thomas for less than two years, starting at $28,000 annually, leaving (for reasons never made public) despite a salary which had risen to $75,000.[12] Lasker, however, found a worthy replacement in Claude C. Hopkins, who started in 1908 at $185,000 yearly, and who, among other accomplishments, educated America to the notions that Quaker puffed cereals were "shot from guns," that Schlitz beer bottles were "washed in live steam," and that Lucky Strike tobacco was "toasted"— the first claim a pure fabrication, and the latter two standard industry practice.[13] (Precisely how these triumphs exemplified "Reason-Why" advertising still eludes me, but so does a great deal about early twentieth century America.)

As early as 1897, Hopkins had been preaching the hard-sell gospel. "I consider advertising as dramatic salesmanship," he said repeatedly. "Advertising must be better than ordinary argument, just as a play must be stronger than ordinary life."[14] While Kennedy moved on to comfortable retirement, Hopkins continued to spread the word:

> Frivolity has no place in advertising. Nor has humor. Spending money is usually serious business. . . . Money represents life and work. It is highly respected. . . .
>
> Never seek to amuse. That is not the purpose of advertising. People get their amusements in the reading-matter columns.
>
> The only interest you can profitably offer is something people want.[15]

(Perhaps a clue to the nature of early twentieth-century America may lie in the notion that people could be *amused* by the reading matter in their newspapers.)

As the dominant, or perhaps merely best-publicized, purpose of advertising shifted from informing and attracting to hard-sell persuasion, ad creation replaced media buying as the agency's major activity, although not its source of profit, since the standard compensation system remained commission on space purchased. Gradually, however, advertising men began to view themselves as serious practitioners of the art of mass manipulation. World War I provided an exquisite opportunity for the rising profession to place its talents in the service of the national propaganda effort. America's first modern public opinion machine, the Committee on Public Information (CPI), headed by journalist-editor George Creel, has been aptly described as "a gargantuan advertising agency the like of which the country had never known."[16] Creel himself, in his memoir evocatively entitled, *How We Advertised America,* noted that the morale-building, falsehood-fighting, patriotism-instilling efforts of the CPI were "so distinctly in the nature of an advertising campaign . . . that we turned almost instinctively to the advertising profession for advice and assistance."[17] The admen were, by and large, happy to oblige, and spent the war simultaneously vending victory, Americanism, and White Owl cigars by showing a smiling, puffing doughboy alongside the caption, "We smash 'em *hard,*" and Ivory Soap, which:

> follows the flag. Wherever Americans go, it is "among those present." Ivory is as unchangeable a part of American life as the practice of cleanliness itself. Ivory Soap is, in fact, the very joy of life itself to Our Boys when they are relieved from the front lines for rest, recreation, and a bath.[18]

Between the propaganda of the CPI and the commercial tie-ins of consumer advertising, World War I probably provided as fine an example of the Reason-Why Approach as the Republic had ever seen.

Following the Armistice, advertising mercifully returned to more purely commercial, though hardly less effusive, pursuits, refining its techniques and reaching perhaps the apogee of its classic period in a series of ads for a rather unexceptional product in search of a redeeming use.

"We went into Marion's office," wrote Gerard Lambert several decades after the event, "and I closed the door. I announced that we would not leave the room until we had an advertising idea for Listerine."

The colloquy began.

> For a long time we batted ideas around. Marion spoke up apol-
> ogetically. "How about bad breath?" he asked. I glared, remind-
> ing him that this was a respectable meeting. Once more he
> brought it up. Impatiently, to get rid of the subject for good, I
> yelled over the low partition to Mr. Deacon and asked him to
> come in.[19]

After appropriate consultation, Mr. Deacon went out and returned with a clipping from *The Lancet*, a British medical journal. The item in hand dealt with the problem of halitosis.

> I interrupted, "What's that?"
> "Oh," he said, "that is the medical name for bad breath."
> Mr. Deacon never knew what hit him.[20]

Having chosen the disease, Gerard Lambert hurried downtown, bought a picture of a pretty girl, rushed back, and captioned it, *Often a bridesmaid but never a bride.* Subsequent ads expanded the theme. If poor Edna couldn't get a husband because of halitosis, nobody wanted to talk to Marvin, *The prince of pariahs,* at all. Other ads featured forlorn, anonymous women who stared at photos of their men and wondered, *Why had he so changed in his attentions?,* and equally melancholy males who pondered the rapid promotions of colleagues and speculated, *Maybe it's my breath.*

The product sold exceptionally well. The fear-and-trembling sociodrama style soon spawned a host of imitators, and the 1920s became the great era, not only of halitosis, but also of bromodosis (sweaty foot odors), acidosis (upset stomach), homotosis (lack of attractive home furnishings), *Tinea Tricho-
phyton* (athlete's foot), B.O. (body odor), and "lazy intestines" (a defect easily fixed by regular dosages of Fleischmann's Yeast, a product whose sales had been declining since the

advent of commercially-baked bread).[21] Lambert, for his part, subsequently expanded the curative properties of Listerine to include dandruff, pneumonia (if taken in time), and assorted other ailments, real, potential, and imaginary. Still, such advertising did provide a useful service, alerting the populace to both imminent perils and readily-available cures, as well as the socio-sexual benefits accruing therefrom. Indeed, such beneficence may well have been part of what Calvin Coolidge had in mind when he remarked that:

> Advertising ministers to the spiritual side of trade. . . . It is a great power which is inspiring and ennobling the commercial world. It is all part of the great work of the regeneration and redemption of man.[22]

(And lest anyone think this attitude confined to those of the Republican persuasion, even Franklin Roosevelt avowed that: "It is essentially a form of education; and the progress of civilization depends on education.")[23]

And so it was, for the adman of the 1920s offered far more than Listerine. Due in part to his wartime experiences, and due in part to a phenomenon to be discussed shortly, the adman had, as Otis Pease puts it, "come to think of himself as an instiller of 'ideas,'" and gladly took upon himself *la mission civilisatrice* of American business.[24] Not content with mere commercial hyperbole or Chamber of Commerce effusion, Bruce Barton of the BBDO agency marketed a commodity which, even by the prevailing standards of Babbitry, seemed a bit excessive. Calling Christ the greatest businessman who ever lived, Barton wrote admiringly of the Saviour's sense of enterprise. "Somewhere, at some unforgettable hour, the daring filled his heart. He knew that he was bigger than Nazareth."[25]

But Christ was more than just some spiritual entrepreneur filled with "consuming sincerity" and organizational acumen. The Messiah portrayed in Barton's best-seller, *The Man Nobody Knows*, also understood the dynamics of the advertising game:

> Take any one of the parables, no matter which—you will find that it exemplifies all the principles on which advertising text books are written. Always a picture in the very first sen-

tence; crisp, graphic language and a message so clear that even
the dullest cannot escape it. . . . Every advertising man ought to
study the parables of Jesus.[26]

No doubt some did. But not enough, apparently, and his-
torians of the trade have little to say about the Depression
years. Recent scholarly studies, however, have noted a rather
complex response. According to Roland Marchand in his
excellent volume, *Advertising the American Dream*, basic appeals
didn't undergo any fundamental changes during the Depression. However, the tone of 1930s advertising did tend to
become more strident, and Depression tie-ins (the need to
economize, the importance of first impressions in business,
etc.) became considerably more explicit and brutal as the bad
years lengthened. Simultaneously, ads played upon the need
for courage and determination (what Marchand calls "the
clenched-fist style of advertising"), and also offered periodic
soliloquies on conquering the slump. Notes Marchand:

> Corporate leaders appreciated the circulation of inspiriting mes-
> sages within narrow business circles; but they looked even more
> favorably upon those businesses, agencies, and publishers who
> bought advertising space to help restore optimism (and gener-
> ous buying habits) to the public as well. . . . The advertising
> journals welcomed each inspirational message with pathetic
> gratitude. When the Packard Motor Company ran an anti-
> hoarding ad that proclaimed "To buy today is a patriotic duty,"
> *Printer's Ink* offered the company effusive congratulations on its
> unselfishness.[27]

Unfortunately, a massive shortage of consumer dollars and
a sustained barrage of consumerist criticism could not be quite
so easily conquered. Advertising didn't end the Depression.
World War II did, and, as Geoffrey Perrett has aptly phrased
it: "Advertising was the war's most curious growth industry."[28] Volume soared, even for advertisers whose production
facilities had been given over to the war effort; since advertising expenditures remained deductible business costs, lavish ad
campaigns could both keep a company's name before the public and soak up excess war production profits. So advertisers

sold not only their wares (when they had them), but also the war, and, perhaps more importantly, the postwar cornucopia.

The straining for tie-ins to all three often grew ludicrous, and occasionally offensive to the men overseas. Recounted cartoonist Bill Mauldin:

> We [the GI's serving in Italy] all used to get sore at . . . some of the ads we saw in the magazines from America. . . . I remember one lulu of a refrigerator ad showing a lovely, dreamy-eyed wife gazing about the blue seas and reflecting on how much she misses Jack. . . . BUT she knows he'll never be content to come home to his cozy nest (equipped with a frosty refrigerator; sorry, we're engaged in vital war production now) until the . . . world is clear for little Jack's son to grow up in. . . . Like hell Jack doesn't want to come home now. And when he does come home you can bet he'll buy some other brand of refrigerator.[29]

Even the arms makers drew occasional flak:

> One advertisement was headed, "Who's Afraid of the Big Focke-Wulf?" [a German fighter plane] All the bomber pilots at one combat field in ETO signed it, *"I am,"* and sent the clipped magazine page back to the manufacturer.[30]

In fairness, though, it must be noted that Madison Avenue also turned out some reasonably tasteful and effective stuff.

But advertising is, after all, essentially a peacetime activity, and peace provided the industry with a welcome opportunity to take up where it had left off in 1929, as the expositor of and guide to an economy of seemingly endless abundance. "If an advertising man," concluded *Business Week* in 1952, "tried to dream up the best of all possible worlds for himself, he could hardly improve on what he has got right now."[31]

But even the best of all possible worlds is complex, and the long-awaited golden years of the 1950s had another, less attractive side—a side several decades in the making by the time it became an issue of national concern.

HUCKSTERS AND
PSYCHOLOGISTS

A man who says that men are machines may be a great scientist. A man who says he *is* a machine is "depersonalized" in psychiatric jargon. Such persons are rightly regarded as crazy. Yet why do we not regard a theory that seeks to transmute persons into automata or animals as equally crazy?

R. D. Laing
The Divided Self

People Have Become "Standardized" by Advertising
1920 Headline in Printer's Ink

During the nineteenth and early twentieth centuries, advertising evolved from an essentially local phenomenon into an activity of national stature and scope. Along the way, a new class of professionals arose: commercial mass persuaders and manipulators in the service of a large-scale corporate economy. The adman of the 1920's clearly understood the basic requirement of those who had hired him—sell their goods. But such had always been the overt function of the ad, whether defined as news of product availability or Reason-Why high pressure salesmanship. What made the advertising of the early twentieth century new was not so much a change in purpose as in process and in social and cultural effect, a change much more profound than a simple switch from "news of the store" to "salesmanship in print" or on the air.

For several decades prior to the 1920's, advertising had responded to the imperatives of an economy in which production increased by quanta, consumption by seeming droplets.

Indeed, mass advertising owed its very existence to the conundrum of devising a distribution and sales system that could keep pace with gains in productivity. By the early twentieth century, many admen recognized the correction of this imbalance as perhaps their major ongoing economic and social task: to sell with steady efficiency and thereby to provide a vital support to an industrial system increasingly troubled by the vicissitudes of the business cycle.

In this endeavor, the advertising profession found willing help.

If capitalist economics gave advertising its *raison d' être,* less tangible forces shaped its themes. In essence, early twentieth-century advertising began to respond, not only to the economic pressures of mass production, but also to a basic reorientation of American thought and culture which started roughly in the 1890s, achieved full expression over the next five or six decades, and has yet to run its course. Viewed in extremely simplistic terms, this change involved a new conception of the individual: his nature, his needs, his reasons, his world and the means by which these might be manipulated and controlled. These new models of human life, and the rudimentary technologies of manipulation and control, came from that curious hybrid of rigor and fog, the modern social and therapeutic sciences, and by the 1920s advertising, which served the needs of corporate America with techniques that earlier generations might have found, to say the least, disquieting.

The 1890s endured the first installment of what later generations would call a crisis of confidence: a diffuse, nagging sensation that older verities no longer offered either transcendent authority or practical guidance for an advanced, urbanizing, ethnically diverse, industrial society. Morton White has called this time of troubles "the revolt against formalism." More sweepingly, Henry F. May has labelled it "the end of American innocence."[1] However interpreted, one result of this decades-long uneasiness stands out: "the rise," as Thomas L. Haskell puts it, "to cultural dominance of the social sciences in the late nineteenth and early twentieth centuries."[2] Into the authority gap created by the new complexities and uncertainties of life came a number of nascent disciplines and pseudo-disciplines which (at least in theory and in self-advertisement) purported both to examine and minister to the human mind with the methodologies of the natural sciences. And, just as physical science had found practical expression in the technology of mass production, so did the social and therapeutic sciences apply themselves to mass production's problems of human engineering.

At first, the social and therapeutic scientists (or, more exactly, those who either hired on or had their insights co-opted) aided the physical engineers in the rationalization of production by scientific management. But, early in the twentieth century, numbers of these social and therapeutic scientists (mostly psychologists), began to subject distribution and consumption to the same scrutiny and manipulation they had applied to the human side of work. In both cases, the objective was the same.

Efficiency.

The entry of the professional psychologist, that scientist/therapist *par excellence*, into the field of advertising paralleled and complemented his growing influence in the areas of production management and industrial psychology. What David S. Noble has called the second industrial revolution began when the worker and, more slowly, the white-collar operative, having been stripped of autonomous skills, were redefined as human cogs, and therefore as objects fit for manipulations designed to increase their "adjustment" and hence their efficiency. As industrial production became as much a matter of human co-ordination as of material technique, there occurred "a shift in engineering focus from the natural to the social, from productive forces to social relations."[3] Stated simply, the problem was no longer what fragment of a task the employee might perform, but getting him to work regularly, on time, and in a reasonably quiescent frame of mind. One possible partial solution to this problem entailed persuading the individual to conceive of himself primarily as a consumer of mass-produced goods, rather than primarily as a producer, a unionist, an anarchist, a Christian, a Republican, or whatever. Two benefits would accrue to the corporate economy: a tractable and presumably nonrevolutionary work force and increasingly dependable mass consumption. And this, ultimately, is what advertising, *as a self-conscious profession employing specific techniques of persuasion, manipulation, and therapy*, set out to do in the decades prior to the Great Depression. By the 1920s, concludes Otis Pease:

> the world of the advertisement had become distinctly more complex. Passing gradually from simple methods of emotional and nonrational appeal, national advertising attempted to traffic in beliefs concerning the good life.[4]

As ever, the overt mission of the individual ad remained the same: to sell. And, as ever, the great bulk of advertising, and perhaps the overwhelming majority of advertisers and their agencies, remained more concerned with day-to-day, bottom-line results than with the arcana of psychological theory and technique. But advertising, *as a professionally coherent institution*, moved beyond mere paeans to the produce and high pressure appeals aimed at rational self-interest, and began to redefine values and offer social and cultural guidance in ways calculated to spur consumption. That this could happen at all was due, in large measure, to increased interest in advertising by a number of influential professional psychologists, gentlemen then in the process of discarding nineteenth-century "faculty psychology," with its emphasis on rationality and will, for the newer vision of behaviorism: a vision of man as a reactive, irrational, haphazardly conditioned, endlessly malleable organism.

Now, to be sure, the entire profession did not participate instantly in this kind of thing, and it was not until the 1950s that *Business Week* could write of the "torrid love affair" between advertising and psychology.[5] But by the 1920s, the apparatus of psychologically-based mass manipulation was in place and functioning.

The first applications were crude. Columbia University's Albert T. Poffenberger offered up as psychological erudition an "Inventory of Human Desires," among which Thirst stood first, followed by Hunger, Sex, and Comfort, with Conformity and Difference in positions seven and eight, respectively.[6] While some admen might quibble with Professor Poffenberger's ratings, finding Conformity and Difference perhaps more useful than Thirst, and Sex an all-purpose consumption motivator, others could not but be gratified by the frontispiece of Professor Walter Dill Scott's *Psychology of Advertising* (1908):

> The author respectfully dedicates this volume to that increasing number of AMERICAN BUSINESS MEN who successfully apply Science where their predecessors were confined to Custom.[7]

Noting that "I have never seen or heard any reference to anything except psychology which could furnish a stable foundation for a theory of advertising," the generally-acknowledged founder of advertising psychology (and future president of Northwestern University) proceeded to emphasize not just the economic necessity of matching consumption to production, but also the pathetic helplessness of the consumer, upon whose habits and whims great corporations ultimately depended:

> Alas, alas, that the day of the self-sufficient and competent purchaser has passed! . . . When the woman of the house steps to the telephone to order provisions of the morrow, she is haunted with the visions for the unseen world—microbes, poison, adulterations and substitutions. . . . It is quite beyond her power to judge of the quality or the value of all her purchases. . . .
> The buyer of an automobile . . . is unable to judge for himself as to the quality of material and workmanship that goes into his vehicle of transportation.[8]

Advertising, according to Scott, needed to reassure and instruct the millions caught in a double bind: adrift in a world without verities save manufactured goods, yet also utterly unable to assess those goods in any rational way.

This is 1908.

With the later contributions (hired or co-opted) of other experts, such as John B. Watson, founder of the American school of behaviorism (who, after his dismissal from the Johns Hopkins University, ended up on the J. Walter Thompson payroll), and Floyd H. Allport, conceiver of the notion that a person's self-image consists largely of his images of others' images of him, advertising found itself in possession of some novel paradigms. Specifically, these were a set of theories and techniques based upon the assumptions that, within the human mind, irrationality, insecurity, and malleability predominated, and that these minds could be induced to clamor ceaselessly for the output of an industrial society *as a source of private meaning, self-comprehension, and therapy.* Almost from the beginning of the century, concludes one student of the subject:

> advertising increasingly appealed, not to the rational judgment of the potential buyer, but to the emotional and nonrational elements in human beings; the Good Life replaced the Good Product as the salable commodity.[9]

But, the Good Life as defined by whom?

THE COMMODITY SELF

Modern man, if he dared to be articulate about his concept of heaven, would describe a vision which would look
like the biggest department store in the world.

Erich Fromm
The Sane Society

To thrive and spread, a consumer culture required more
than a national apparatus of marketing and distribution;
it also needed a favorable moral climate.

T. J. Jackson Lears
From Salvation to Self-Realization

There is in logic an error known as the fallacy of composition,
which consists of attributing to an aggregate the characteristics or effects of its component parts. If, for example, a man
saves half his income, he generally grows more prosperous
and secure. If an entire society saves at that rate, the result is
a depression catastrophic for all. To understand the significance of advertising, it is necessary to discard at the outset an
almost instinctive exercise in the fallacy of composition. An
individual ad, whatever its style or effectiveness, is rarely
regarded as an intrinsically significant part of the universe.
From this admittedly correct perception flows the apparently
logical conclusion that advertising as an aggregate contains
nothing more than an enormous amount of trivia.

Not so. For nearly a century now, the whole has been
rather more than the sum of its parts.

To recapitulate:

By the 1920s, advertising, as a decentralized but nonetheless self-conscious, professionally organized, and cohesive
institution, served an industrial system generating ever greater

quantities of merchandise. Increasingly, also, the advertising profession drew upon the services and expertise (co-opted and/or hired) of another class of professionals: social and therapeutic scientists, especially psychologists, and especially those whose concept of *homo sapiens* corresponded roughly to the adman's vision of the ideal consumer: rootless, insecure, ignorant, a malleable product of social conditioning, amenable to whatever stimuli the advertiser might care to associate with his product.

To be sure, it wasn't, and isn't, quite as simple or effective as that. Ask any advertiser. Ask any retailer. Consumers have always been notoriously fickle and unreliable, and advertising has yet to reach a level of manipulative or therapeutic competence that can guarantee consistent, predictable success. (Most probably it never will.) As that old advertising cliche, attributed to numerous sources, has it: Half the money spent on advertising is wasted, but nobody knows which half. Even the great John B. Watson, embarking on his second career as the J. Walter Thompson agency's resident behavioral psychologist, discovered this fact of life rather quickly. As Stephen Fox relates the tale:

> "To make your consumer react," Watson promised his advertising colleagues, "it is only necessary to confront him with either fundamental or conditioned emotional stimuli."
>
> Upon joining the agency, he was sent through the usual training program. For ten weeks he made his rounds selling Yuban coffee to grocers; he spent another two months as a clerk in a department store. "I saw I would have to more or less junk my psychological training," he noted. His academic learning included nothing about industry or consumer tastes.[1]

What Dr. Watson discovered was what every advertising professional knows only too well: The only relevant consumer response to the advertiser's stimuli is cash-defined, and usually damnably hard to induce. However, the issue here is not whether any particular advertisement or campaign works; the issue is advertising as a coherent form of discourse. And this coherence was, and is, provided largely by the social and therapeutic sciences. Well over half a century ago, psychologists began to augment age-old techniques of blandishment with their insights and pseudo-insights, while advertising professionals melded them to the economic imperatives and personal turmoils of capitalist civilization.

And, for the first time, advertising offered itself as a *guide to life.* Advertising professionals began to evolve (as Marchand puts it) "from salesmen to confidantes."[2]

Hitherto, advertising had done its work by rational persuasion, legitimate puffery, outright fraud, or all three. An ad might promise the lucky purchaser everything from sex appeal to immortality, but the ad itself, once it had done its work (or failed to do so), lost both meaning and significance. In the early twentieth century, though, by virtue of increasing quantity and evolving technique, and also by the diminution of other, more traditional forms of guidance, advertising, *as an aggregated phenomenon,* became a significant factor in the nation's social, cultural, and ethical life, simultaneously reinforcing the values of mass production and altering the environment itself in favor of those values. This "propaganda of commodities," as Christopher Lasch describes it,

> serves a double function. First, it upholds consumption as an alternative to protest or rebellion. . . .
> In the second place, the propaganda of consumption turns alienation itself into a commodity. It addresses itself to the spiritual desolation of modern life and proposes consumption as the cure.[3]

In the early twentieth century, this propaganda of consumption—what Michael Schudson aptly labelled "capitalist realism"—first came into its own as a means of social engineering and control.[4]

Just as the purpose of mass advertising cannot be understood outside of its economic context, its effects cannot be understood outside of their social, cultural, and ethical contexts. Mass production requires mass markets. Standardized goods require standardized tastes, desires, and needs. Industry provides the first; advertising tends to the final three.

In a provocative, albeit somewhat flawed, little volume, *Captains of Consciousness,* Stuart Ewen has traced the development of advertising's social, cultural, and ethical activities and roles. Ewen's work suffers from three methodological shortcomings—none of which, however, negate either his thesis or his conclusions. First, he tends to blur the line between professional coherence and outright conspiracy. Psychologically-based and therapeutic advertising may indeed have been the trade's *avant-garde* during those years; they were never universally accepted or practiced.

Second, Ewen takes his sources a bit too literally. Drawing on the speeches and writings of those advertising professionals and high-level business executives who saw advertising as a means of social control is necessary, of course. However, Ewen never seems to realize the extent to which these men might simply be hyping their wares and themselves. He tends, in short, to equate what they claim they can do with what they're actually doing—always a dangerous practice.

Third, as Schudson points out, it hardly seems reasonable to believe that advertising could defuse and assuage social tensions at the bottom strata of society.[5] A bit above that level, yes, but advertising, for obvious reasons, has little interest in addressing those with little money. Thus, those social and economic strata most likely to revolt would also be the least affected by advertising, except perhaps as a further inducement to hatred.

Still, *Captains of Consciousness* provides a good sketch of both a force at work and the perceptions of those who created and evaluated it. Based upon detailed scrutiny of the speeches and writings of the profession's early practitioners and spokesmen, Ewen argues that, while each ad strove primarily to vend its particular commodity, advertising as institution and process did indeed try to inculcate consumption as both alternative to and antidote for personal unhappiness, class consciousness, and social change:

> The advertising which attempted to create the dependable mass
> of consumers required by modern industry did so by playing
> upon the fears and frustrations evoked by mass society—offer-

ing mass produced visions of individualism by which people could extricate themselves from the mass. The rationale was simple. If a person was unhappy within mass society, advertising was attempting to put that unhappiness to work in the name of that society.[6]

Toward that end, advertising developed a style and a repertoire of appeals which aimed at the creation of what Ewen calls the "Commodity Self": a conception of personal and collective existence in which one defines oneself and others primarily by consumption of patterns, and in which everyone addresses the dilemmas of modern life with a single, all-purpose solution:

Buy something.

To the "Commodity Self," neither the system nor the soul could be held responsible for disasters, failures, inadequacies, or malaise, since the remedy for everything lay close at hand in consumption. Personal defeats or disappointments could thus be defined as lack of purchasing power, and communal inequities as nothing more than unequal access to consumer goods. "The use of psychological methods," writes Ewen," . . . attempted to turn the consumer's critical function away from the product [and the system] and toward himself."[7] But toward himself in a very limited sense: toward himself as failed consumer, not as inadequate human being or victim of unjust arrangements.

And this was the message which the advertising of the period hammered home: consume for the sake of temporal salvation, of metamorphosis, of authenticity, of meaning on earth. A random sample of the ads of the early twentieth century, and certainly those of the 1920's and 1930's, confirms that they keyed heavily and openly on what miracles a product could work for one's advancement, either by providing one with some indispensable personality adjunct, or else by instantly correcting some interior flaw. Professor Marchand has gone so far as to label these ads "parables" and "icons"— genres of which the Listerine ads discussed above were only one example.[8] Further, by equating the "Good Life" not so much with wealth *per se* as with constant business, social, and personal advancement via constant consumption, advertising attempted "the elevation of the goods and values of mass production to the realm of a *truth.*"[9] (Ewen's italics.)

Ironically, however, the major target of this campaign was neither the working class nor the growing middle stratum of society *per se.* Instead, advertising mounted a more general assault. "To create mass consumption, advertising had to develop concepts of good which cut across other lines."[10] It had to target the one institution which, although already much weakened by industrial capitalism, still claimed some remnant of autonomous authority, and which also disposed of the dollars that the advertisers coveted.

That institution was the family.

Industrial capitalism, by the twentieth century, had largely stripped the urban family of its productive functions by moving work from the home into the factory or office. With that co-optation substantially complete, the next step entailed redefining the family as primarily a consuming unit—a tiny group of persons with radically different interests and life-styles, united on a day-to-day basis by little more than acts of common consumption. "While sociologists lamented the loosening bonds of family life," contends Ewen, "the businessmen in the twenties saw the phenomenon as an essential part of their own rise to dominance. . . . Business was to provide the source of a new life style, where before father had been the dictator of family spirit."[11]

This redefinition, according to Ewen, took three interlocking forms: the elevation of youth and youthfulness to the status of a salable ideal, the equation of female liberation with skillful consumption, and the recasting of sexual activity and sexuality itself as primarily consumption-based and consumption-defined phenomena. Now, youth and sexual satisfaction are generally considered desirable conditions, and have been since man discovered that their opposites—old age and frustration—were somewhat less pleasant affairs. But never before had the deification of these items been seen as an unending source of corporate profit. And never before had these two tempestuous conditions been co-opted by one organized sector of society (non-totalitarian society, at any rate) and then employed to weaken the authority and structure of society's primary institution, the family . . . in the name of that society's prosperity and well-being.

Advertising did not create such changes alone, of course, nor with anything approaching total effectiveness. What advertising did attempt to do was to co-opt and to codify pre-existing and ongoing processes of change within American culture, and then to use them for private profit. It did so within the context of new styles of thought, new personal liberties, new forms of behavior, and new uncertainties: changes occurring at the highest intellectual levels as well as in the back seats of model T's on Saturday nights. If advertising tried to redefine father as the quasi-comic provider of disposable income, mother as the quintessential manager of consumption, and youth as the ideal toward which all, including their elders should strive, it did so as part of a society which had already made such redefinitions plausible. If advertising attempted to use the ideas and techniques of the social and therapeutic sciences in order to gain its economic ends, it did so as part of a society that had already cast off other forms of authority, guidance, and truth. If the adman of the 1920s offered himself as both expert in and therapist for modern life in an increasingly large-scale, impersonal world, if he vended values along with his merchandise, he did so as part of a culture that had already acquiesced in similar usurpations by other professional groups. In an age stripped of verities, but deluged with expertise, the adman fit in very well.

He was, according to his lights, a kind of social therapist.

PART TWO

THE SYSTEM EXPANDING

THE FIFTIES...
AND A CAVEAT

What, then, is the nature of the Madison Avenue villain?
We must conclude that he is not villain at all. He is
an agent of this system, not its founder, and though he
profits by it, he cannot be held ultimately responsible
for it.

Robert Brustein
The Madison Avenue Villain

I would suggest that the destiny of our Western civilization turns on the issue of our struggle with all that Madison Avenue represents, more than it turns on the issue
of our struggle with Communism.

Arnold Toynbee
Quoted in Time Magazine

It was, for advertising, the best of times and the worst of times.
In the 1950s, thanks largely to a burgeoning economy, the
new possibilities of the electronic media and changing demo-
graphics, advertising enjoyed unprecedented profitability and
ubiquity. Yet it was also the object of a great deal of caustic
scrutiny, much of it coming from within the profession itself.
As always, critics faulted advertising for its espousal of "mate-
rialism"—a venerable criticism, somewhat akin to criticizing
a football player for aggressiveness or a model for concern
with her appearance. But many more critics, from university
professors to admen themselves, found advertising's greatest
offense in its insufferable banality, its never-ending *badness*.

Most advertising of the 1950s was, indeed, wretched, a fact caricatured by former adman Joseph J. Seldin:

> The man of the house arose that morning and brushed the rich, creamy lather into his stubble and got a perfect shave as usual. It left his face soothed and refreshed. On other mornings he used an electric razor which also delivered supreme shaving comfort. . . . At breakfast he greeted his wife with a good-morning kiss as she handed him a glass of juice to help him fight fatigue, colds, and maintain his alkaline balance all day. There was wholesome goodness in every sip.[1]

It was this kind of advertising which prompted agency head David Ogilvy to remind his colleagues that "the consumer isn't a moron; she is your wife." Another successful adman, Jerry Della Femina, sneered that "the people who're doing the ads are often as stupid as the people they think they're talking to."[2]

But underneath all the banality, three important changes were taking place. As psychology grew more complex, so did advertising's uses of it; both moved beyond simple stimulus/response behaviorism to exploitation of Freudian and ego psychology insights and pseudo-insights. The second change was that the proliferation of virtually identical consumer products (cars, cereals, toys, etc.) required that advertising engage more heavily than ever before in "marginal differentiation," emphasis on minor-to-imaginary product distinctions. This growing need helped create a new "Brand Image" philosophy to compete with the older, hard-sell "Reason-Why" school. Finally, the advent of the Baby Boom generation created a unique opportunity not only to exploit a new market, but also to train from birth a whole cohort of consumers.

Despite these changes, however, it is possible to see the advertising of the 1950s as less a break with the past than a continuity. In *The Mirror Makers,* for example, Stephen Fox argues that little in advertising ever really changes, except cyclically. There exist, after all, only a finite number of appeals—hard-sell versus soft-sell, product benefit versus user benefit, etc.—and whatever the psychological fashions, the essential repertoire remains the same. Further, it should be noted (one final time) that the vast majority of advertising is relatively straightforward, and far from posing as guidance, therapy, or anything else. But what concerns us here are the changes, the often rather subtle changes, and not the relatively stable mass. And perhaps it would be useful to conceive of the evolution of advertising by borrowing an analogy from Freud:

> . . . suppose that Rome is not a human habitation, but a psychical entity . . . an entity, that is to say, in which nothing that has once come into existence will have passed away and all the earlier phases of development continue to exist alongside the latest ones. This would mean that in Rome the palaces of the Caesars and the Septizonium of Septimius would still be rising to their old height on the Palatine and that the castle of S. Angelo would still be carrying on its battlements the beautiful statues which graced it until the siege of the Goths, and so on. But more than this. In the place occupied by the Palazzo Caffarelli would once more stand—without the Palazzo having to be removed—the temple of Jupiter Capitolinus; and this not only in its latest shape, as the Romans of the Empire saw it, but also . . .[3]

And so on. At the time he penned this display of antiquarian erudition, Freud was speaking of the development of the human mind. But the analogy is apt. In advertising, as in the minds it seeks to influence, the oldest and the newest often share the same space. And in the 1950s, that space came to include both new kinds of manipulation and new kinds of people to manipulate.

FASTER THAN THE
EYE CAN SEE

Not the adventurer . . . not the exploiter . . . not the "robber baron"—but the *consumer is king today.*
> S. H. Britt
> *The Spenders*

Just where does one draw the line beyond which others must not be allowed to influence one's inner life?
> *Bruno Bettelheim*
> *The Informed Heart*

Someone once observed that American consumers are a lot like bacteria. The more you dose them, the greater resistance they develop. In the 1950s, this problem became acute. True, advertising was now ubiquitous, thanks to the commercialization of television and the resurrection of radio via rock-and-roll. But what could motivate consumers so deluged, literally inundated by all-but-identical advertisements for all-but-identical products? In short, as the need for effective manipulation grew ever greater, the ads all seemed to be canceling each other out. As much in desperation as curiosity, admen began to investigate the possibility of bypassing the consumer's conscious mind entirely. In 1957, two events—a press conference and a book's publication—brought these methods to public light, and a brief but intensive furor ensued.

On September 12, 1957, James Vicary, Vice President of the Subliminal Projection Company, Inc., announced that his concern had perfected a device whereby commercial messages might be intermixed with normal viewing material and flashed on a movie or television screen at speeds too rapid for the conscious mind to perceive. The subconscious, however, could and did pick these messages up. Vicary went on to disclose the results of an experiment conducted at an unnamed New Jersey movie theatre. Commercials urging the unsuspecting patrons to drink Coke and eat popcorn had been so projected—with gratifying results at the concession stand. Although pleased by success, the inventor was not unaware of his gadget's disturbing implications. Vicary himself, reported Gay Talese in *The New York Times,*

> believes that his invention should be regulated, "either by the industries which use it or by the government. . . ."
>
> He explains that he had spent many years developing the process because he realized that commercial television would eventually reach the point where there would have to be excessive use of commercials in order to satisfy the advertisers' demands for time.[1]

Subliminal projection, Vicary felt, offered a reasonable compromise between commercial requirements and viewer convenience.

Amid mass pronouncements of alarm, the government and the advertising industry moved to investigate, and Vicary soon found himself in the unenviable position of having to denigrate his invention's effectiveness in order to survive professionally. At a Washington D.C. demonstration on January 13, 1958, Vicary assured the assembled lawmakers, F.C.C. representatives, and media types that subliminal projection could never compel anyone to act against his own beliefs or preferences. "'It may,' he announced, 'cause a Coke drinker to drink more Coke . . . but it won't get him to switch to Pepsi.'"[2] The guests at the special screening of *The Gray Ghost* (*cum* subliminal ads) agreed. One spectator observed that "'I hated popcorn before, and I still do,'" while Senator Charles E. Potter, Republican of Michigan, was quoted as stating to a colleague during the demonstration: "'I think I want a hot dog.'"[3]

Through much of 1958, a curious *pas de deux* of public alarms and industry disclaimers continued. *Life Magazine* ran an article (apparently written by a certain Herb Brean) which periodically interrupted the text with the fine-print message, *Marilyn Monroe, Call Herb Brean.*[4] The authoritative Advertising Research Foundation, however, could have spared him the trouble, for six months later it announced that it had reviewed the evidence and authoritatively termed it "insufficient."[5] Television station KTLA in Los Angeles first announced and then abandoned plans to offer subliminal services, while Congressman William A. Dawson, Republican of Utah, expressed concern that "a proposed new form of television advertising might make beer drinkers out of unsuspecting teenagers."[6]

By year's end, however, the issue was all but forgotten, and in a 1962 post-mortem, *Advertising Age* revealed that the Subliminal Projection Company, Inc., had folded, and that inventor Vicary had found employment with Dun and Bradstreet.[7] Indeed, the whole issue burned out as suddenly as it had flared, a demise which might call into question the terror with which *The Nation* had denounced the gadget as "the most . . . outrageous discovery since Mr. Gatling invented his gun."[8] But, whatever the nature of the furor, it does seem certain that Vicary's machine would never have received so much attention, were it not for the publication, earlier in 1957, of Vance Packard's ominously entitled exposé, *The Hidden Persuaders.*

THE HIDDEN PERSUADERS

> For we have shown that persuasion must in every case be effected either (1) by working on the emotions of the judges themselves, (2) by giving them the right impression of the speakers' character, or (3) by proving the truth of the statements made.
>
> *Aristotle*
> *Rhetoric*

> After they are done with their shopping, people often feel vaguely disappointed . . .
>
> *Ernest van den Haag*
> *What to Do about Advertising*

It sold.

And, *mirabile dictu,* it's still in print today.

Whatever Vance Packard's motivations for writing *The Hidden Persuaders,* he read his market well. "His book," concluded Ernest van den Haag, "caters to our insatiable appetite for the 'inside story,' an appetite spawned by the obsessive American fear of being manipulated by hidden forces."[1] To charges of sensationalism, alarmism, and irresponsibility, Packard later replied:

> My main defense is that the efficacy of the [psychological] techniques described was not, frankly, my main concern. Techniques can be perfected. . . . My concern was with the fact that these techniques, whatever their validity, *were even being attempted* on the public.[2] (Packard's italics)

By exposing the machinations of the "Hidden Persuaders"— those advertising researchers and practitioners who went beyond behavioral psychology into the realms of psychoanalysis and the various ego or "depth" psychologies—Packard suggested that he was performing a necessary, indeed laudable civic task.

Perhaps. Certainly in a society as saturated with advertising as 1950s America, the task needed doing. But, as Elmo Roper reported, the Persuaders were far from Hidden.[3] The theory and practice of Motivation Research (M.R.) had been openly debated for nearly a decade before Packard's volume appeared in 1957. Within the advertising profession, a truly vitriolic opposition, usually spearheaded by Alfred Politz, a prominent statistical researcher, contested and condemned anything so nebulous as probing and manipulating the consumer's unconscious. (Of course, Politz was also defending his own professional interests by denigrating M.R.) Nor did the popular and professional periodicals lack for copy on who was engaged in the dissection of the consumer's intrapsychic (as opposed to overtly behavioral) process, and what uses could be gleaned from the shards of insight so revealed.[4] What Packard did was to survey the new techniques via largely public sources, conduct an interview or two, deftly package his findings, and then, with all the acumen of the manipulators he deplored, sell the product to a public alternately alarmed and titillated by the excesses allegedly revealed.

"This book," began *The Hidden Persuaders,*

> is an attempt to explore a strange and rather exotic new area of human life. It is about the large-scale efforts being made, often with impressive success, to channel our unthinking habits, our purchasing decisions, and our thought processes by the use of insights gleaned from psychiatry and the social sciences. Typically these efforts take place beneath our level of awareness. . . . The result is that many of us are being influenced, far more than we realize, in the patterns of our everyday lives.
>
> Some of the manipulating being done is simply amusing. Some of it is disquieting, particularly when viewed as a portent of what may be ahead on a more intensive and effective scale

for us all. Co-operative scientists have come along providentially to furnish some awesome tools.[5]

Drawing almost entirely on open sources, Packard proceeded to analyze the "subterranean operations of the depth boys."[6] From trade journals and text books he discovered that M.R. asks not only *what* the consumer wants, but also *why*, and further assumes that the consumer's surface, i.e., rational, answer is not usually the true one. Confiding that the depth boys see us as "bundles of daydreams, misty hidden yearnings, guilt complexes, and irrational emotional blockages," Packard at times seemed almost to agree with M.R.'s cardinal tenet that, in dealing with human beings, rationality will get you nowhere:

> We are image lovers given to impulsive and compulsive acts. We annoy them [the depth boys] with our seemingly senseless quirks, but please them with our growing docility in responding to their manipulation of symbols that stir us to action.[7]

For two hundred pages, Packard detailed the means by which the symbols that stir us to action are determined, co-opted, and used. *The Hidden Persuaders* bestowed instant notoriety—and a certain measure of credibility—on the hypotheses that convertibles represent mistresses, while hardtops symbolize wives (memo to car dealers: put convertibles in the showroom but stock hardtops); that fountain pens are phallic symbols (memo to males: better invest in a good one); and that home-baked cakes serve as a pregnancy substitute, so instant mixes should allow the housewife to express her creativity ("You Add the Eggs"). In a manner reminiscent of Walter Dill Scott and Albert T. Poffenberger (neither of whom appears in Packard's book), *The Hidden Persuaders* itemized "Eight Hidden Needs" which the depth boys turn to commercial advantage:

1) Emotional Security
2) Reassurance of Worth

3) Ego Gratification
4) Creative Outlets
5) Love Objects
6) Sense of Power
7) Sense of Roots
8) Immortality

And, according to Packard, it all added up to the merchandising of a "packaged soul."[8]

Or, perhaps, a Commodity Self.

In either event, Packard's *Persuaders* had several remarkable aspects. First, leaving aside the author's utter confusion among the non-economic, the unconscious, and the irrational aspects of purchasing behavior, the book made a great deal of money. Ironically, by publicizing the activities of the depth boys, Packard also increased the aggregate demand for their services. "Packard succeeded," wrote Raymond A. Bauer, "in painting the picture of psychological demonology so persuasively that motivation researchers are now concerned with giving their clients a more realistic picture of what they can do."[9]

But of greater interest here are the book's omissions. Not only did Packard appear utterly unaware that psychologically-based commercial manipulation had been going on, in one form or another, for over half a century; he also seemed (despite disclaimers) unable to grasp the implications of the existence of the system. Indeed, he reduced the whole problem to a kind of evasion. Praising the depth boys as "mostly decent, likable people, products of our relentlessly progressive era," he concluded that

> most of them want to control us just a little bit, in order to sell us some product we may find useful or disseminate with us a viewpoint that may be entirely worthy.
>
> But when you are manipulating, where do you stop? Who is to fix the point at which manipulative attempts become socially undesirable?[10]

Packard never answered his own question, suggesting instead that individuals might simply choose not to be persuaded—a contention that ignored his whole point that M.R. was supposed to operate beneath conscious levels. Further, his conclusion exemplified the fallacy of composition. For the real problem was not M.R. per se, but rather the ongoing, cumulating effects of a psychologically-based system now generations old. By failing to recognize this, Packard in effect conceded the high ground to the depth boys . . . and in particular to the man whom he himself had nominated for the title, Founding Father of Motivation Research.

THE STRATEGY OF
DESIRE

This is one of the very definite purposes of advertising: to
help the consumer become articulate about his buying
choices, to put words in his mouth which sound convinc-
ing, even if they are not the right words.

Pierre Martineau
Motivation in Advertising

We are living through the experience of a closed world.

Jacques Ellul
Hope in Time of Abandonment

It was Freud's great achievement to demonstrate that the irrational has structure, and that from its lowest levels may arise
man's highest aspirations and achievements. Between this discovery and Ernest Dichter's espousal of "irrationality in the
service of legitimate goals" lies a philosophical and moral
chasm.[1] Philip Rieff once referred to Freud as "the statesman
of the inner life," convinced that "reason cannot save us,
nothing can; but reason can mitigate the cruelty of living, or
give sufficient reasons for not living. Beyond the training in
lucidity, no healing is honest."[2]

According to Ernest Dichter, Ph.D., onetime Freudian lay
analyst and subsequent motivation researcher: "A long stick
of salami can give the illusion of security and safety, for there
are many slices that can be cut from it."[3]

In the history of psychologically- and psychotherapeutically-based advertising, Dichter stands as both midpoint and
exemplar. As a midpoint, he provides a bridge between the

rudimentary behavioral usages of the early twentieth century and the more complex functions of post-Vietnam-era manipulations. As an exemplar, he typifies a basic shift in American culture, away from the "rationally therapeutic" and toward the more diffuse. The therapeutic advertising of the early twentieth century had keyed upon certain well-defined needs: for specific guidance, for advancement, for accomplishment. They spoke to what might be called the simple form of the Commodity Self. But with Ernest Dichter, advertising began to move beyond this simple form—a package of anxieties and desires of rather traditional mien—and began a complex melding of private emptiness and corporate profitability. Although this shift from "real-world" guidance and assuagement to therapy for empty souls, would not reach fruition until the 1970s, with Ernest Dichter, Ph.D., the change became real.

Ernest Dichter, President of the Institute for Motivational Research, Inc., appears throughout *The Hidden Persuaders* as Packard's archetypal depth boy: "Mr. Mass Motivations Himself."[4] Packard, however, confined his assessment of Dichter's significance to a series of vignettes. It was Dichter, for example, who told the candy bar people to make their product in bite-size, detachable pieces, thereby offering the guiltily self-indulgent consumer the illusion that he could, at his discretion, save some for later. It was Dichter who told the bankers that, if they wanted to lend more money, their ads had to portray the borrower in the morally superior position, thereby relieving vestigial Puritan uneasiness concerning debt. It was Dichter who told the prune people that their product required massive image overhaul, who recommended changing the product's name from "prunes" to "the California Wonder Fruit," and who recommended ads encaptioned, "Put Wings on Your Feet."[5]

En passant, Packard also mentioned Dichter's basic daily rate (during the 1950s) for coming up with the aforementioned and other insights: $500.[6]

But Ernest Dichter, Ph.D., was more than a consultant who commanded some rather hefty fees. He was also a writer; in fact, Packard gleaned many of his more scandalous revelations from Dichter's articles and other publications. And, in the aftermath of the boost which Packard had given Dichter's career, the Freudian-turned-depth boy increased his literary output considerably.

As early as 1947, Dichter had been spreading the gospel that "we are only scratching the surface. In making marketing decisions, we are relying on surveys based on what people say they think and feel."[7]

In 1949, he wrote:

> A purchasing decision is seldom a direct or immediate result of an advertisement. A number of intermediary processes take place in the mind of the potential buyer. Before the sales effectiveness of an advertisement can be known, its psychological impact must be known . . .
>
> In other words, the closer any advertisement comes to producing thoughts which have the appearance of a purchasing act or which rehearse use of the product, the higher the commercial value of the effect of the advertisement.[8]

Sound, common-sense psychology; Professors Scott and Poffenberger might well have approved. But Dichter added a new dimension to the art of psychologically-based manipulation:

> *The actual merchandise is a secondary. Advertising's goal has to be the mobilization and manipulation of human needs as they exist in the consumer.*[9] (Italics minc)

And what Dichter considered the primary need of modern Americans he made absolutely clear in a 1951 *Business Week* article entitled, "You Either Offer Security or Fail."[10]

Security, however, could come in many forms. At the simplest, case-study level, it could be the concept of Betty Crocker as "Mom's *Fuehrer*." According to Dichter: "When a housewife buys a brand of cake mix recommended by such a 'personality,' she has the illusion that she is buying from some one with whom she has a personal relationship—a super-mother whose advice cannot be ignored because she is so powerful."[11] (This is illusion indeed because Betty Crocker never existed.) At a somewhat more abstract level, it could mean any ad's ability to "Resolve the Misery of Choice" or "Provide Moral Permission" for self-indulgence.[12] Whatever the specifics, though, Dichter's concept of security never wavered. He saw it as a triad (or perhaps a trinity), a relationship between consumer goods, the modern soul, and the adman as omnipresent manipulator of both.

Now, physical objects do indeed possess symbolic and affective values. Men die for crosses, flags, or, as Napoleon once sneered, little scraps of ribbon. But when symbols come to overshadow the realities they represent, the result is either fetishism or idolatry. For Dichter, though, merchandise had its own higher meaning. On the one hand, things are the relentless foe:

> As modern life becomes more complex, the struggle with the world around us becomes more and more a relentless cold war [Note choice of analogy]. The army of the enemy is enormous. It ranges from a blown fuse or a run in a stocking to dirt on the floor, from a flat tire to a lost collar button.[13]

And yet:

> [T]he knowledge of the soul of things [Again, note choice of analogy] is possible a very direct and new and revolutionary way of discovering the soul of man. . . . The more intimate the knowledge that a man has of many different types of product, the richer his life will be.
>
> At the same time, the development of this new approach *might well lead to new possibilities of therapy* . . . .[14] (Italics mine)

In sum, then, Dichter grounded his practice in a truism and a claim. The truism, that things have intrapsychic as well as real-world values, formed the basis of his commercial technique. By employing the methods of depth psychology and psychoanalysis, he claimed to identify inner values and anxieties and subsequently manipulate them to the advertiser's

advantage. Toward that end, Dichter published a volume entitled *Handbook of Consumer Motivations,* a compendium of
insights such as "Mystery surrounds cheese" and "Asparagus,
because of its peculiar shape, easily acquires a phallic significance."[15] Presumably by emphasizing these mysterious and
phallic attributes, the prudent advertiser would stay in tune
with the consumer's unconscious, thereby increasing sales.

But Dichter also, and in this context more importantly,
claimed for consumer goods—as interpreted by his technique—an absolute moral and philosophical significance. In
the modern world, he argued, goods (as perceived through the
advertisement's tutelage) had acquired a new meaning. Not
only had there arisen an historically unprecedented supera-
bundance of things, but there now existed, according to
Dichter, a new kind of human being to perceive, relate to, and
purchase those things. Dichter's basic claim, then, was that his
method provided more than a means of doing nice things to
the sales curve; it also offered whole new forms of self-vali-
dation to the people whose dollars and loyalties the advertisers
coveted.

In the 1950s, this new species of American generally went
by the name "Middle Majority," a phrase apparently coined
by social anthropologist W. Lloyd Warner. One distinguishing
feature of this group was a chronic excess of disposable
income, coupled with a relative paucity of ideas on how to
dispose of it. By functioning as a guide to the inchoate and
usually unconscious strivings of these prosperous perplexed,
an advertiser could garner for himself both their unconscious
gratitude and their real-world patronage. In his professional
summa, a volume entitled *The Strategy of Desire,* Dichter wrote:

> Whereas the permanent member of the middle class depends
> largely upon personal relationships in order to decide upon
> household goods that would be appropriate to her class mem-
> bership, the recent member of the middle class turns to imper-
> sonal sources. . . .
>
> Thus, the recent middle-class member does not and indeed
> cannot depend upon the primary channels for the communica-

tion of traditional values, the instructions of parents, relatives, and friends for acquiring the knowledge necessary to her new role.[16]

This did not mean, however, that the advertisement should function, as it had for decades prior, as a mere manual for conventional status-seeking. Rather, it must actively participate in helping the "Middle Majority" discover itself:

> While it is true that the new middle-class must study new values and absorb them, it is also true that, to some extent, where the recent and the permanent middle class members come into contact and intermingle, traditional middle-class values may be modified. . . .
> Traditional symbols of status and prestige are being replaced by modern symbols of status and prestige.[17] (Dichter's italics)

And, according to Dichter, the newest ultimate source of status and prestige, and the most promising stratagem for the canny advertiser, was the marketing of "self-expression." Whereas in the early 1950s he had pushed security, by the early 1960s something quite different had emerged. The trappings of security and status still mattered, but Dichter now argued that they sold less efficiently than the marketing of psychologically-tailored consumption patterns which provided the individual with a mass-produced sense of uniqueness. His rationale was evocative. "There are so many continuing crises," he wrote in 1960, "that we have become crisis-immune. We have decided it is safer to live in capsules of individual isolation."[18] The wise advertiser, therefore, should target these capsules with barrages of product-mediated self-expression, offering satisfactions leading to the following illusion: that consumption-based self-expression could serve as therapy for all the insecurities engendered by social mobility, excess disposable income, isolation, desolation, and, of course, the Russians and the Bomb. Indeed, for Dichter's new "middle majority," fearful of the world and uncertain of its own values, products could acquire a significance which could only bless the advertiser's bottom line. So certain was Dichter that the identity and self-expression needs of the "middle majority" constituted advertising's "New Frontier" that in a *Harvard Business Review* article he asserted:

> We are rapidly reaching a stage, not the least as a result of successful advertising, where the consumer asks, in effect, not just how long the washer will last, but what it will do for his "soul."[19]

And "soul," as used here, had a meaning as specific, and as limited, as security:

> Many of our studies have shown that people are groping for real values and discovering that they lie primarily in self-development and in the realization of self-potential. . . . To the extent that the modern advertiser can tie in this trend with a new car, new refrigerator, or even a new form of cigarette or tonic for tired blood, he will outshine his competition.[20]

For Dichter, then, it all fit together: consumer self-expression, corporate profit, and the advertisement as a bridge between. The method: the use of psychological and psychoanalytic insights to relate advertised illusions of merchandise to certain forms of perceived human aspiration. The market: a new class of human beings, affluent, bewildered, insecure, self-encapsulating. This is the simple "Commodity Self" of the early twentieth century updated, using merchandise and illusion not simply as aids to advancement and happiness, but as the very basis of self-definition. Gerard Lambert may have promised a great deal to those who gargled with his mouthwash, but he never suggested that it might cleanse their souls . . . or provide them with new ones.

Dichter did. And whatever misgivings he may have felt about his livelihood, they didn't show. Indeed, he normally concluded his how-to-do-it publications with passages of almost metaphysical character and messianic intensity, posturings which might have been dismissed as ludicrous were it not that Dichter's handiwork permeated American society. In 1960 he avowed that:

> We must use the modern techniques of motivational thinking and social science to make people constructively discontented. . . .
>
> Many of the anxieties and discontents of modern man are the result of lack of goals . . .[21]

Advertising, as part of comprehensive social engineering, could help manufacture and distribute the necessary aspirations:

> It is too difficult a job to determine one's goals in isolation. Goals in the moral and spiritual field have to come from the country as a whole.
>
> I am suggesting that such a goal can be determined by taking our psychological definition of the goals of life and applying these principles to our country as a whole. . . . *The real test of the political and economic success of the American way of life is whether it does provide this feeling of growth, self-realization, and achievement.*[22] (Italics mine)

Not growth, self-realization, and achievement, but the feelings thereof. For Dichter the instilling of these sensations came to resemble a psychotherapeutic crusade:

> It has become the task of the behavioral scientist—the professional changer of human nature—to point out first that his profession is practiced not because it is better for the economy or because it will result in the achievement of some moral or religious goal but because it helps us reach the basic, eternal summit of human achievement—the Olympian goal of happiness.[23]

Thus Ernest Dichter, Ph.D., in 1971, on the benevolence of his profession in helping mankind attain "basic summits" of Olympian happiness—the same man who, sixteen years before, had informed the Pan American Coffee Bureau that:

> Something has happened to coffee. Because of its universal acceptance and the fact that most people like coffee, we have at the same time been lulled into a complacency about it. . . . Thus, when we are asked how can we increase coffee consumption, our answer is: by helping people rediscover coffee in all its many facets. . . . We feel that every one of the specific questions, such as how to get people to drink more coffee, to take more coffee breaks, to start drinking coffee at an earlier age, etc., are all in one way or another dependent upon this revitalization of coffee which we have set forth as the most immediate objective.[24]

Perhaps, indeed, taking more coffee breaks might help humanity reach the "basic summit of Olympian happiness." Or perhaps, as T. S. Eliot once characterized the modern situation: "I have measured out my life in coffee spoons."

In the matter of spoons, however, Dichter counselled that the trend was away from sterling and toward "a growing tendency to use materials that require little care, such as stainless steel . . . ."[25]

IDENTITY

Ego identity (psychoanalysis): A person's experience of himself as persisting essentially unchanged as a continuous entity through time as a result of the function of the ego which synthesizes one's ideals, behavior, and societal role.

Dictionary of Behavioral Sciences

Safety consists in mastering a battery of taste preferences and the mode of their expression.

David Riesman
The Lonely Crowd

With the advent of motivation research, advertising moved partway from the simple behavioral techniques of the twentieth century's first half and into more modern and subtle realms. The transition to the new, diffuse, therapeutic advertising would not be completed until the 1970s (if indeed it has been completed at all). But by the mid–1960s, the use of Freudian and other depth psychological insights and techniques for commercial manipulation was a firmly established part of the advertising trade.

And yet, there is something a bit awry, a bit "out of sync" here. In the writings of Ernest Dichter one finds an oddly ahistorical quality: an oddness related to both the past and the future. Like Vance Packard, Ernest Dichter seemed utterly unaware that psychologically-based manipulation had been going on for half a century and with a strong therapeutic cast. Perhaps Dichter chose not to mention it in order to enhance the "newness" of his own product, which it was, of course, not.

But in another sense, Dichter's product was astonishingly new. Dichter did the bulk of his work in the 1950s and early

1960s, before counterculture, the search for "commitment," and "do your own thing" became fashionable among the more affluent of the baby boom generation. Yet Dichter ascribed this quest *to their parents,* i.e., to a generation usually portrayed as eminently conformist, self-satisfied, and dull.

Plus ça chance?

By the time Dichter brought Freud to Madison Avenue, however, orthodox Freudian psychoanalysis had long been something of a closed system. True, Freudian theory, with its emphasis on the unconscious and the omnipresent influence of sexuality, seemed peculiarly well-suited to commercial co-optation. On a case-by-case basis, it might work; all the notions about convertibles, fountain pens, asparagus, and cake mixes seemed to have some usable validity. But in the realm of serious psychological thought, the "action" had moved beyond strict Freudianism into the more diffuse realms of neo-Freudian and ego psychology, which emphasized questions of identity and coherence over matters of neurosis, repression, and tyrannical sexuality. As Erik Erikson, one of the leading ego psychologists and (apparent) father of the phrase, "identity crisis," wrote:

> To condense it into a formula: the patient of today suffers most under the problem of what he should believe in and what he should—or, indeed, might—become; while the patient of early psychoanalysis suffered most under conditions which prevented him from becoming what and who he thought he knew he was.[1]

In other words, advertising in the 1950s and early 1960s found itself selling to people who were not only uncertain of their own identities, but also not really all that different from each other. In their ambitions, frustrations, and habits, the post-World War II "middle majority" displayed a remarkable homogeneity.

As did the products they used. In the years before Vietnam, the central problem of selfhood and the central problem of marketing began to converge: *how to create, define, and sustain individual identity in a world troubled not only by a seemingly endless array of possible choices, but also by the basic sameness of so many of the competing entries.*

THE GREAT DEBATE

Advertising, in addition to its purely informing function, adds a new value to the existing value of the product. But the fact that the value is fictitious as perceived by the consumer does not mean that it is unreal as enjoyed by the consumer. He finds a difference between technically identical products because the advertising has in fact made them different.

> Martin Mayer
> *Madison Avenue U.S.A.*

And in our faults by lies we flattered be.

> William Shakespeare
> *Sonnet 138*

In the late 1950s and early 1960s, a debate of almost academic intensity burst the confines of Madison Avenue and entered the public domain. The protagonists, both of whom doubtless enjoyed the publicity immensely, were among the profession's most successful agency heads. Both men claimed sole possession of the secret of good advertising. And even though neither man held a high opinion of sophisticated, psychologically-based manipulation, both men grappled with an essentially psychological problem: how to provide merchandise with "identity."

"Few disagreements in any business," reported Martin Mayer in 1958, "have been so thoroughly thrashed out as the conflict in viewpoint between [David] Ogilvy and [Rosser] Reeves." The rivalry was all-encompassing:

Each regards the other as a great personal salesman; each shakes his head over the way the other wastes his clients' money. . . . Competitive with each other both personally and professionally, they conduct their competition within the framework of a mutual admiration society.[1]

With the publication of Reeves' *Reality in Advertising* (1961) and Ogilvy's *Confessions of an Advertising Man* (1962), the controversy turned literary.

The basic dilemma of modern advertising, Reeves once told Mayer, was that few products really differed from their competition in any significant way:

> Our problem is—a client comes into my office and throws two newly-minted half-dollars onto my desk and says, "Mine is the one on the left. You prove it's better."[2]

In order to prove the superiority of the coin on the left, Reeves developed the concept of the Unique Selling Proposition (U.S.P.), an idea in one sense no more than a revival of old-fashioned "Reason-Why" advertising, but in another sense quite different. "Reason-Why" advertising concerned itself with rational (albeit usually hyper-enthusiastic) appeals to consumer self-interest; U.S.P. worked in the realm of identity.

Central to the U.S.P. theory is the proposition that "the consumer tends to remember just one thing from an advertisement—one strong claim or one strong concept."[3] What the consumer ought to take away from the ad, therefore, is the one best impression of the product: one Unique Selling Proposition.

Reeves delineated his theory as follows:

> 1. Each advertisement must make a proposition to the consumer. . . .
> 2. The proposition must be one that the competition either cannot, *or does not* offer. It must be unique—either a uniqueness of the brand *or a claim not otherwise made* in that particular field of advertising. . . .
> 3. The proposition must be so strong that it can move the mass millions. . . .[4] (Italics mine)

Anything other than a real U.S.P. constitutes mere puffery, futile wordsmithing, or distractive window-dressing. And that, according to Reeves, is just about all most advertisements are: "Technically, these advertisements dance and shine. It's just that they have no real content. We find that we are sifting through chaff looking for wheat. In the middle of all this, drop a real U.S.P.: 'STOPS HALITOSIS!' The U.S.P. almost lifts itself out of the ruck and wings it way to some corner of the mind."[5]

For Reeves, then, advertising meant "the art of getting a Unique Selling Proposition into the heads of the most people at the least possible cost."[6] (Speaking of heads, perhaps Reeves' most famous commercial was for Anacin, which showed individual boxes of pain and tension banging, sparking, and knotting away inside a cartoon head. Luckily, however, Anacin contained "the pain reliever doctors recommend most" . . . aspirin.)

Reeves had a point with his U.S.P. gospel. Given the competitive clutter of the market and the media, and the sameness of the entries (both products and ads), all else had to take second place to that one essential aspect of the average product which the adman had to identify or fabricate, and then burn into the consumer's already inundated mind.

In contrast to Rosser Reeves' neo-Reason-Why approach, David Ogilvy favored a more subtle style. Ogilvy, a Scottish immigrant who had tried his hand at Oxford, *haute cuisine,* tobacco farming, opinion polling, and espionage (World War II service with the British embassy in Washington) before co-founding his own agency in 1948, dedicated his practice to the concept that:

> Every advertisement should be thought of as a contribution to the complex symbol which is the *brand image*. . . .
>
> The greater the similarity between brands, the less part reason plays in brand selection. . . .
>
> The manufacturer who dedicates his advertising to building the most sharply defined *personality* for his brand will get the largest share of the market . . . .[7] (Ogilvy's italics)

It worked well enough for Ogilvy to become the adman exemplar of the 1950s and early 1960s, and indeed some of the most pleasantly sophisticated advertising of that era came

out of Ogilvy & Mather. Perhaps the two most famous applications of Brand Image theory were the incarnation for
Schweppes of Commander Whitehead (a genuine Schweppes
executive and former Royal Navy officer) as the aristocratic,
slightly enigmatic "Man from Schweppes," come to America
to bring it good things (in this case, "Schweppevescence"),
and the Hathaway campaign in which Ogilvy put an eye patch
over a Russian *emigré* aristocrat's perfectly functional right
eye. "Exactly why it turned out so successful," Ogilvy later
ruminated in print, "I shall never know."[8] Lack of detailed
knowledge did not, however, prevent Hathaway from suddenly dominating the shirt market, or Ogilvy from engaging
in an act of advertising *hubris* which left the competition both
envious and annoyed. So well-known had the Hathaway model's eyepatch become that Ogilvy felt justified in spending his
client's money on a *New Yorker* ad containing neither words
nor trademark—just the Hathaway-shirted, eyepatched Baron
Wrangel, working beside a telescope.[9]

And yet, despite the apparent polar differences between
U.S.P. and Brand Imagery, two broad similarities did exist.
Reeves readily conceded that a U.S.P. need not always take the
sledgehammer approach, citing with admiration Clairol's
"Does she . . . or doesn't she?" proposition.[10] And Ogilvy, for
his part, acknowledged that:

> When we advertise Shell, we give consumers *facts,* many of
> which other gasoline marketers *could give, but don't.* When we
> advertise KLM Royal Dutch Airlines, we tell travellers about the
> safety precautions *which all airlines take, but fail to mention* in their
> advertisements.[11] (Italics mine)

In sum, then, the advertising of the pre-Vietnam years
evolved in three inter-related ways. First, its quantity
increased exponentially and, courtesy of television and popular radio, advertising became, for the first time, truly omnipresent. If a great deal of this advertising was frightfully bad, perhaps that was due simply to the fact that, in any business, the
need for talent usually exceeds the supply. No doubt, too,

some of it was the fault of excessively censorious networks and timid clients, seeking the approach that would alienate the fewest people.

But of greater importance was the increased use of psychological and psychotherapeutic insights and techniques which placed less emphasis on crude stimulus-response and overt guidance and more on the problems of identity formation. To repeat: *in the years prior to Vietnam, the central problem of personality and the central problem of marketing began to coincide.*

But more than this. Since the early years of the century, advertising had extolled the virtues of youth, and used the young in order to increase consumption. The process had been uneven, periodically interrupted by war, depression, and the artificially low birth rates they occasioned. But in the years after World War II, the advent of the Baby Boom gave advertising its first opportunity to train an entire generation of consumers from birth—in effect, to create the ultimate dependable mass market. And in the 1950s and early 1960s, the prospect seemed attainable.

There was, after all, peace, prosperity, and no end to good times in sight.

THE TRAINING OF
THE YOUNG

But if the alienated [young] lack clear affirmative goals
and values, they nonetheless share a common search in a
similar direction. Among their goals are honesty, direct
confrontation with unpleasant truth, unflinching awareness of evil—implicit in their rejection of pretense,
hypocrisy, self-blinding rationalizations and self-serving
defenses.

Kenneth Keniston
The Uncommitted

Desires of young people are more plastic than those of
older persons.

C.H. Sandage
Advertising: Theory and Practice

Few aspects of advertising have aroused more general debate
than the effects of intensive manipulation of the young. A vast
critical and technical literature, ranging in style from the statistical to the vitriolic, addresses the subject. Insights and con-
demnations abound. Conclusions, however, do not, and the
ongoing analysis of the exact significance of the fact that X%
of children aged Y to Z actually think relief is spelled R-O-L-A-
I-D-S continues to elude us all.

Whatever the disagreements, however, three facts constitute the basis of any historical inquiry. First, an unprecedented
youth market did develop during the 1950s and 1960s. Second, advertising both recognized and acted upon the short–
and long-term potential of this market. And third, the
response of this market—this generation—was, from the

advertiser's point of view, a stunning success with seemingly
limitless potential. To be sure, individual products might fail;
many did, especially in the volatile areas of youth-oriented
amusements, foods, and clothing. But the structuring of the
youth market as a coherent, enduring entity did indeed come
about, and continues to evolve today.

The postwar baby boom, roughly defined as including
those born between 1946 and 1964—about 76,441,000 people—provided the advertising industry with its first opportunity to work on an entire generation, almost literally from
birth, and under extremely favorable conditions.[1] Times were
prosperous; radio and television removed the constraints of lit-
eracy; all ages and educational levels could now be targeted.
And indeed, by the mid 1950s, almost no sentient American
could exist for more than a few hours without exposure to
commercial communication. This new omnipresence, coupled
with the general presumption of perpetually self-sustaining
affluence, augured unlimited possibilities for those with the
tools to exploit them. "Just look at youth!" gushed one how-
to-do-it manual:

> No established pattern. No backlog of items. No inventory of
> treasured and, to many an adult's way of thinking, irreplaceable
> objects. Youth, from the time he is carried proudly down the
> hospital steps to the time he marries and renews the cycle, is the
> greatest growing force in the community. His physical needs
> alone constitute a growing requirement in food, clothes, enter-
> tainment, etc. It has definitely been established that because he
> is open-minded and desires to learn, he is often the first to
> accept new and forward-looking products.[2]

To the admen, the mere existence of this new generation
seemed promising in several ways. The marketable needs of
the pre-teen set might be relatively small, but the size of the
cohort resulted in instant prosperity (followed, in the 1970s,
by equally swift depression) for such items as diapers, baby
food, etc. True, toddlers disposed of little independent income,
but every Sunday morning moppets by the millions absorbed

several hours of a televised catechism: *Be the first kid on your block to . . .* or *Say, kids, when your mom goes to the store, tell her to . . . ad infinitum* and *ad nauseam*. And again, the possibilities inherent in mass came into play—products sold at a nickel or a dollar each, but sold by the millions every year. And, as the toddler matured (to be replaced by imitative younger siblings), and as tastes and allowance expanded, a wider range of merchandise could be promoted. This generally took two forms: unique teen and pre-adult items, contributing to the nascent youth culture, and also the pre-selling of fully adult items. Teens and pre-teens might not, for example, usually buy their own cars, but they could be both presold and used as a powerful influence upon parental buying decisions. At its simplest, this strategy entailed what Joseph Seldin called the art of "turning children into the extended selling arm of the advertiser."[3] Writing in 1953, he reported with some dismay on

> the research findings of the Youth Research Institute that "youngsters eagerly repeat television and radio commercials over and over again." Assurance is offered advertisers by the Youth Research Institute that "millions of youngsters in homes throughout the nation are singing the merits of advertised products with the same vigor displayed by the most enthusiastic announcers." An additional bright spot is that a catchy commercial is repeatedly sung during the day by youngsters at no additional cost. "They are also much more difficult to turn off," the report adds.[4]

For this approach, the syntax of 1950s and early 1960s advertising—simple jingles, meaningless superlatives, puerile slogans more memorable for inflection than for content—worked extremely well. Further, since brand loyalty is usually an irrational (or only partly rational) affair, and since children had little or no comparative information on which to base their assessments, less-than-adult resistance would be encountered. Indeed, children often demonstrated intense loyalties to products they had never tried, and perhaps could not even recognize, describe, or understand. Reported one adult advertising professional:

> Speaking of surveys, we tried an experiment the other evening. . . . To a curly-headed four-year old being tucked under the covers we posed this question: "Susie, which product brushes teeth whiter?" "Colgate's, of course, Gramp." We couldn't resist another. "Which product washes clothes cleaner?" "Tide." We tried once more. "Which coffee gives the best value?" When she replied, "A and P, and now good night, Gramp," we hurried out of the child's room with other questions beating at our brain.
>
> Where else on earth is brand consciousness firmly fixed in the minds of four-year old tots? How many pre-school age Americans are presold on how many different products? What is it worth to a manufacturer who can close in on this juvenile audience and continue to sell it under controlled conditions, year after year, right up to its attainment of adulthood and full-fledged buyer status? It *can* be done. Interested?[5]

This approach—preselling the kiddies—constituted the basic tactic. At a somewhat more sophisticated level, advertisers could use children within their commercials, thereby providing the youthful viewer with someone as well as something to identify with, and drawing *en passant* upon a widened range of adult affective responses.

"The arena in which children's advertising could operate," suggested one consultant," is vast, encompassing any product which could conceivably be geared to a children's market."[6] For example:

> Instead of an appeal based on fear, insurance companies might stress positive elements, such as educational insurance. Show two children, say, talking about how great they are going to be when they grow up, because Daddy is going to buy a special policy.[7]

Presumably, the child, equating his own future accomplishments with Daddy's insurance, would be moved to make inquiry concerning the family estate. Daddy, for reasons of his own, would respond in some actuarially appropriate manner.

As a further benefit, the child might acquire an abiding insurance consciousness which would repay the advertiser handsomely a few decades down the road.

But if merry jingles served to introduce myriad products to the tots, and slightly older children could be induced to pressure their parents in a variety of subtle and not-so-subtle ways, the predominant youth market tactic was simply a quantum expansion of a generations-old industry offering: benevolent therapeutic guidance. For over half a century, advertising had offered itself as a guide to competence in life. But while the adults might require counsel in numerous specific areas, the juveniles needed it in only two: how to cope with the *Sturm und Drang* of adolescence, and how to gain that *sine qua non* of teen-aged existence, popularity. It worked. As David Riesman once remarked: "The product now in demand is neither a staple nor a machine; it is a personality."[8] To an astonishing degree, the emerging youth market keyed upon this need, offering consumption and consumption patterns as the royal road to acceptance, the guaranteed solution to problems and crises, and a never-failing source of therapy.

But did the kids believe it? True, the Baby Boom generation might have been content to define itself according to consumption patterns, i.e., according to the dictates of consumer society. But this does not necessarily imply genuine faith in the curative powers of consumption, or in the adult world which so assiduously manufactured and marketed the cures. Thousands of studies have confirmed that by the teen-age years (if not earlier) almost all children learn to discount advertising claims about 100%. But what about the world which manufactures those claims? While researching his book, *Madison Avenue U.S.A.*, Martin Mayer interviewed an advertising executive who related the following story. It is worth quoting in full, not only for what it reveals, but also for what it foreshadows:

> "My children know I'm in advertising, but it doesn't interest them. They don't ask me about it. The other day, though, we were all watching television, and one of those cartoon commer-

cials came on. It showed two big wrestlers coming into a ring, one with the label PAIN on his robe, and the other with the label ORDINARY PAIN KILLER. Something like that. Anyway, PAIN threw ORDINARY PAIN KILLER right out of the ring and stomped around afterward. Then another wrestler came on, with this brand name stencilled on his robe, and he threw PAIN out of the ring, knocked him completely out, you see.

"I didn't think much of it, one way or the other, but my younger boy called me aside, out of the room. He said, 'Dad, am I to understand that a bunch of grown men sat around and thought up that thing? And another bunch of grown men sat around and said it was a good idea? And another bunch of grown men went to all the work to make a movie of it?'

"What could I say? I told him that was just what had happened. He walked away, shaking his head."[9]

Within a few years, more than heads would be shaking.

PART THREE

THE TRIUMPH OF
THE THERAPEUTIC

CREATIVITY

I think it possible that we may soon even *define* therapy as a search for values, because ultimately the search for identity is, in essence, the search for one's own intrinsic, authentic values.

> *Abraham H. Maslow*
> *Toward a Psychology of Being*

Make ads that people will feel.

> *William Bernbach*
> *Quoted in Advertising Age*

In retrospect, two things, at least, seem clear. First, that the 1960s were a time of unusual intensity. And second, that, for some people, there was a war on.

The intensity can be summarized here. Almost cultic in style (and occasionally in reality), it worshipped the triple gods of identity, authenticity, and experiential intensity. It rejected, or appeared to reject, the latticework of values and habits associated with corporate capitalism and liberal bourgeois ideology. It was both post-modern and anti-modern.

In itself, this rejection was no new American phenomenon. Oddities and geniuses had been trying it for centuries: Ralph Waldo Emerson, Walt Whitman, Henry David Thoreau, to name a few. Nor were the 1960s the first time that such rebellions and such quests had been undertaken by large numbers of people. Writes T. J. Jackson Lears on the late nineteenth-century version:

> By exalting "authentic" experience as an end in itself, anti-modern impulses reinforced the shift from a Protestant ethos of salvation through self-denial to a therapeutic ideal of self-fulfillment in *this* world through exuberant health and intense

71

experience.... Superficially at odds, anti-modernist, avant-gardist, and advertiser have often been brothers under the skin.[1]

And so there were the 1960s, albeit in a more complex sort of way. As the decade began, advertising entered its short-lived Creative Revolution: a period dominated by a few agencies and personalities who produced (let us be honest) some absolutely delightful commercial folk art. In terms of chronology, the Creative Revolution coincided with the Kennedy/ Johnson years, ending sometime in Nixon's first administration. In fact, at the outset, admen often sounded astonishingly "New Frontiersy" in their calls for an end to dull, flat, weary, stale but immensely profitable advertising ("Ask not . . . ") In a 1960 convention speech, BBDO's Charlie Brower reported advertising, like America, "Ready for Renaissance." According to *Advertising Age:*

> Mr. Brower outlined four conditions he said history has shown to be necessary for a creative renaissance. "They usually followed a period of mediocrity; they occurred when there was some feeling of security; everyone, high and low, desired and encouraged the return of greatness; and there was a fierce nationalistic, religious, or group loyalty. . . . "
>
> According to Mr. Brower, "The national desire for greatness is growing in strength daily." Americans, he said, are growing restless about mediocrity.
>
> "People are sick of sameness," he said. "Hungry for new products and new ideas. For dynamic, fresh, and original selling."[2]

Four years later, Young & Rubicam's George Gribbin suggested in a Pittsburgh oration that "the 15th century Renaissance man should be the ideal of the twentieth century advertising man," since both, he pointed out, were "generalists."[3]

And, in the midst of—or, perhaps, in spite of—all the exhortations, the Creative Revolution did indeed get underway: an explosion of authenticity, intensity, and identity. The revolution would ultimately fall victim both to economic recession and a too-eager (in some circles) accommodation to the so-called counter-culture. But, for a few shining years, it seemed as though Camelot had come to Madison Avenue, as well as to Washington, D.C.

The Revolution itself was a three-part affair, the first two stages dominated by established professionals, the third by an ultimately suicidal influx of kids. Phase One, beginning in the latter 1950s and associated largely with William Bernbach of the Doyle Dane Bernbach (DDB) agency, demonstrated that advertising based upon mildly self-deprecating humor, low pressure, and literate copy could both energize sales charts and instill the ads themselves with a certain endearing quality. In his early efforts on behalf of Levy's Bread ("You Don't Have to Be Jewish"), Orbach's Department Stores (talking cats, talking cattily), El Al Airlines ("My Son, the Pilot"), and Polaroid cameras, Bernbach worked minor miracles. But two campaigns—for Volkswagen and Avis—brought the DDB style to such a level of wry sophistication that Victor Navasky could contend in the *New York Times:* "With such credentials, he [Bernbach] can rightfully stake out his claim as advertising's first existentialist."[4]

If Doyle Dane Bernbach dominated Phase One of the Creative Revolution, Wells, Rich, Greene (WRG), and especially the agency's head, Mary Wells Lawrence, controlled Phase Two. By ordinary standards, their success was inexplicable. "Would you invest in this enterprise?" asked the *Wall Street Journal* in 1968, two years after the agency's founding. "It has annoyed the American Legion, enraged the Better Business Bureau of Detroit, and counts among its triumphs an airline whose planes are painted in pastel colors. Its fixed assets consist largely of office furniture."[5] But the WRG triumvirate, on the strength of their work for Braniff (the aforementioned pastel-colored planes, Pucci-clad stewardesses, and the dubious slogan "Does Your Wife Know You're Flying with Us?"), Benson & Hedges 100-millimeter cigarettes ("Oh, the Disadvantages . . . "), and Alka-Seltzer ("No Matter What Shape Your Stomach's In") managed, within a few years, to become Madison Avenue's most spectacularly successful new agency.[6] Not surprisingly, WRG spawned a horde of imitators and helped to inspire Phase Three of the Creative Revolution: the Kids.

Advertising in the 1960s was perhaps the first major American profession to experience the mass entry of the new generation as practitioners. These young people, most of them non-Ivy League, many of them non-college, and more than a few decidedly non-normal, brought their counter-cultural ambience with them, immediately antagonizing their elders by both their impudence and their advertising. Contrary to popular assumption, advertising usually follows the trends at a discreet distance, especially when promoting products with diverse markets. And, it has often been noted, excesses of any kind—language, nudity, deliberate offensiveness—readily tarnish the profession as a whole. But, in the beginning at least, the Kids could be deemed at least potentially a Good Thing. "God knows where they come from," wrote Jerry Della Femina, himself a somewhat older *Wunderkind.* But he considered their presence all to the good:

> It's the kids who are really revolutionizing the advertising business today. It's the kids with nothing to lose. The kids are pushing ahead, mainly because they communicate to consumers like we've never communicated before.[7]

By the late 1960s, many of the Kids were commanding unprecedented salaries, especially when involved in advertising targeting their peers. Many, too, were breaking away to start their own tiny agencies, disparagingly dubbed "boutiques" by the larger establishments which had trained them and whose accounts they often took with them when they left.

At decade's end, however, the bottom fell out, and the great advertising crash of 1969–1970 is, in many ways, astonishingly evocative of the larger cultural situation. By 1969, it had become glaringly apparent that the "Let-the-Children-Lead-Us" phenomenon, whether in politics, morality, culture, or advertising, was leading only to chaos. And, as advertising had been perhaps the first profession to accept (or endure) the new generation as workers, so it became among the first to reinvoke its own standards. Among the casualties of establishment backlash: the boutiques, hundreds of individual careers, and the Creative Revolution itself. And, in the aftermath of the 1960s, advertising repented its go-go years. Ironically, the repentance drove it even deeper into the therapeutic mode, but that's anticipating the story a bit.

It is entirely conceivable that, were it not for Bill Bernbach, advertising might never have known a modern conceptual alternative to its heavy-handed inanity of the 1950s. True, David Ogilvy had produced excellent soft-sell advertising, but (as his critics hastened to point out) usually for big-ticket, luxury goods: Rolls Royce automobiles, KLM air travel, Puerto Rican vacations, etc. Even his campaigns for mundane items such as soda (in this case, Schweppes) strove for an appeal not exactly intended to move the masses. "Great advertising," ran the standard dismissal, "but try to sell something ordinary to the masses with it."

Bill Bernbach did. With DDB's Volkswagen campaign, the advertising profession finally learned that effective advertising could also be wry, honest, and universally popular. And with the campaign for Avis, he proved once again a premise which, pre-Bernbach, had verged on blasphemy: "You've got to be willing to talk about your product disparagingly in order to be believed."[8]

In 1949, Volkswagen sold a total of two cars in the United States. The product seemed utterly preposterous for the American market—a tiny, ugly car manufactured by a recently defeated enemy—indeed, a car which owed its paternity to Adolf Hitler's desire to put every German on wheels. Ten years later, however, consumer curiosity and word-of-mouth advertising by enraptured owners had resulted in a six-month waiting list for cars. Thus, to say that advertising "made" Volkswagen into an American success story is not quite true; the success already existed. But two new factors made 1959 a prudent year in which to begin serious advertising. In Germany, the plant was expanding at an alarming rate, while in the United States, Detroit was preparing to introduce its first competitive compacts. So Volkswagen of America, after some agency-shopping and chance encounters, decided to hire DDB.[9] The German company had three requirements: that the ads be honest, amusing, and not denigrate Detroit. Bernbach agreed.

For DDB, and especially for Bernbach, Creativity did not flow *ex nihilo*. In fact, Bernbach believed in a variant of Rosser Reeves' U.S.P. axiom. But where Reeves drove home his points by sheer repetition, Bernbach used the concept to provide the basic theme, to which Creativity could then be assiduously applied. As he later recounted, a trip to the factory in Wolfsburg, Germany supplied the *leitmotif*. "We knew what distinguished this car. We knew what we had to tell the American public. We had to say, 'This is an honest car.'"[10] Which they did, in an astonishingly (for the era) novel and effective way: perhaps best exemplified by an ad headlined "Lemon."

By capitalizing on the car's utter lack of stylishness, plus its undeniable economy, DDB succeeded in changing the nature of automobile advertising. No paeans to chrome-plated, hyperbolically-tailfinned, insatiably gas-thirsty tonnages of incipient obsolescence—just wry, honest salesmanship. The small car became an American fixture, and the ads themselves bits of commercial folk art as well as the prototype for another campaign, this one on behalf of an obscure concern which hadn't turned a profit in fifteen years.

In a strict marketing sense, Volkswagen and Avis confronted antipodal problems. Where Volkswagen had only to capitalize on a pre-existing and expanding market, Avis' dilemma was simple survival. Recounted one observer:

> Townsend [Avis President Robert C. Townsend] went to half a dozen agencies with this request: "I have $1 million to spend, and I need $5 million worth of impact," and was told to get lost. But when he came to Doyle Dane Bernbach, for some quixotic reason Bernbach told him he would do it for him. He asked for ninety days in which to prepare the campaign. "But you must promise to run everything we write without changing a bloody comma." . . . Townsend promised.[11]

As he'd done with Volkswagen, Bernbach began casting about for a U.S.P. to distinguish Avis, in this case an unenviable chore. Reported *Newsweek* in 1964:

> Robert C. Townsend, the president of Avis, Inc., was talking with his advertising agency about ways to boost his rent-a-car business, which trailed far behind Hertz in the car-rental field. Were Avis' cars newer than Hertz's? asked the admen. No. More rental locations? No. Lower rates? Nope. Wasn't there some difference between the two? "Well," said Townsend, thinking for a moment, "We try harder."[12]

Now, the conventional advertising practice of the era, not to mention business courtesy, dictated that no one ever mention the competition by name. Too many things could go wrong, from legal proceedings to the ever-present danger that the inattentive consumer might believe the ad actually promoted the competition's offering. But having already broken two of advertising's most cherished taboos, against humor and self-deprecating honesty, Bernbach determined to shatter one more. With its combination of shock value and incorrigibly cheerful aggressiveness, the Avis "We're #2 So We Try Harder" campaign succeeded brilliantly, and "We Try Harder" buttons became a fixture of 1960s' American life. (And one button especially, that worn by a Marine machine gunner on his helmet in a famous Vietnam photograph.) And yet, adman/writer Jerry Della Femina suggested:

> According to people I've talked to, the Avis "We Try Harder" campaign by Doyle, Dane Bernbach was never meant to beat Hertz. . . . When the Avis campaign began, Hertz was number one and Avis and National were running neck and neck for number two. But look how clever it was: Avis attacks the guy who is number one and makes it a one-two situation and nobody even remembers that National is still around.[13]

Whatever the strategy, it worked. And with the tandem of spectacular Volkswagen/Avis successes, as *The New York Times* reported, "more and more agencies, rather than risk losing an account to Doyle, Dane, are striving to emulate the style of William Bernbach, the agency's head."[14] Clients clamored for imitation, and prominent among the seekers was, not unexpectedly, Hertz.

Since 1959, the Norman, Craig, and Kummel agency had handled #1, relying on their "Let Hertz Put You in the Driver's Seat" theme. This campaign, which in televised form featured a man in business attire falling out of the sky into a moving convertible, was a prime example of what NCK called their "empathy" approach—a philosophy also responsible for such creations as the Ajax White Knight and the equally empathic White Tornado.[15] When the Avis campaign struck, the initial reaction of both Hertz and NCK was to ignore it, a policy justified by one Hertz executive's sardonic quip that "Avis can live off taking business from us, but we can't live off taking business from them."[16]

By 1966, however, the cumulative effect of the campaign could no longer be ignored, evaded, or denied. As Cary Ally, the man whose agency took over the account, told his new clients: "They're making assholes out of you."[17] Finally, Hertz and Ally decided to strike back openly, and did so in a campaign which not only replicated the DDB style, but which also resembled a World War I trench incident in which a German commander, irate over French propaganda leaflets accusing him of seducing his officers' wives, fired back a barrage of shells containing printed denials.

Still, the Hertz "Get Tough with Avis" campaign did provide a welcome quick fix for both profits and employee morale. The ads ran a mere six months. As Ally later recalled, "It was a once-in-a-lifetime situation, and we had made our point."[18] That point, however, included much more than the concession that DDB-style advertising worked. It also provided a bit of proof that humor and honesty need not be confined to a single agency.

If Phase One of the Creative Revolution belonged to Bill Bernbach and his agency, Phase Two was dominated by the most flamboyantly successful woman in advertising history. "This is our moment," said the Bernbach-trained Mary Wells in 1966 after she, Dick Rich, and Stuart Greene had bolted the Jack Tinker agency to form WRG. "I am not the least bit humble about it," she went on. "In any era, some agencies come along to set new trends, to illuminate the industry in some way. . . . We are the agency of today."[19] And, in fact, WRG did become a prototype, the most publicized of the new agencies. Its boutique stage didn't last long, well under a year, and WRG soon found itself in rivalry with DDB for numbers of clients lining up at the door—a sight which agitated the industry into frozen smiles of jealous admiration. "Well, chaps," began a 1967 *Madison Avenue Magazine* feature:

> you remember where we left our three All-American kids, Mary, Dick, and Stu, perched on all those empty desks in that empty office, smiling bravely at the future while they waited for the telephone to ring . . .
> Of course you remember. Everyone remembers. How, after they got Braniff and Benson and Hedges, they won accounts for American Motors, Bristol Myers, General Mills, Hunt-Wesson Foods, Seagram's, Smith, Kline and French, Sicks' Ranier Brewing, West End Brewing, and Western Union. . . . No agency in history has ever grown so big so fast.[20]

The avenue gaped, and even normally unflappable *Fortune Magazine* paid the trio the unprecedented honor of running two feature articles on WRG in under three years: the first entitled, "On Lovable Madison Avenue with Mary, Dick, and Stew," and the second, "As the World Turns—On Madison Avenue," after Ms. Wells married Braniff head Sterling Lawrence and then dumped the Braniff account . . . for TWA.[21]

But what, precisely, was corporate America lining up for? While DDB offered wry, self-deprecating humor, WRG sold sophisticated whimsicality, or what *Fortune* called "the knack of understated hyperbole."[22] WRG offered an aura so suave that self-mockery seemed the greatest sophistication of all. But while each ad relied on soft-sell chic, total campaigns—and the WRG philosophy of doing business—were aggressiveness incarnate. "Making a little ripple today is nothing," said Mrs. Lawrence in 1969. "It takes a lot to impress today. Spend money and spend it big."[23] In the overheating economy and overheated culture of the latter 1960s, this combination of ambition, acute sensitivity to trend, and considerable female charm worked well with both clients and consumers, and the agency may well have deserved its motto: *If We Were Modest We'd Be Perfect.* Modesty, however, was not among WRG's fixed assets. "We want to make money, of course," Mrs. Lawrence flatly announced. "We want to upgrade our lives by two generations. But the whole point is that we want to produce the most wonderful and exciting advertising that's ever been done. *We want to prove that we are right.*"[24] (Italics mine)

And they did . . . almost. Unfortunately, the WRG style, with its uninhibited trendiness, came to be imitated too quickly and too poorly by too many less-talented practitioners, leaving the industry ill-prepared for the 1969–1970 crash.

If the first phase of the Creative Revolution was dominated by DDB, and the second by WRG, the third belonged to nobody in particular—or, actually, to a bewildering array of new personalities, agencies, and techniques. So extensive was the disarray that *Saturday Review* could conclude: "There would appear to be few businesses, at the moment, in so violent a state of ferment as the advertising agency business."[25] It wasn't all creative ferment, either. The creations and escapades of DDB and WRG may have had their detractors, but the profession both respected and emulated their achievements. Not so with the Kids, the boutiques, and the new counter-cultural/psychedelic appeals. The backlash only waited the proper moment.

Until about 1967, only Wall Street and the old-line law firms rivaled Madison Avenue as Ivy League preserves. Early in the 1960s, however, new faces started appearing, many of them avowedly ethnic, a few non-white. Most of the new arrivals were simply unpolished, ambitious young people, drawn to advertising, as Della Femina and Wells had been, because it seemed like a fun way to make money. But as the decade wore on, other newcomers more closely fitted one writer's sobriquet of "institutional hippies" than the more traditional young man or woman on the make. While this new breed, reported *Marketing/Communications Magazine,* "shares the avant-gardism, Nowism, New-Wave-ism, and basic creativity [sic] . . . of your still undomesticated hippie, there is an important difference. The institutional hippie has the freakishly un-American desire to become rich and famous."[26]

In the beginning, the influx of youth posed no threat to the establishment, and may in fact have provided some rudimentary guidance on how to deal with and co-opt emerging cultural trends. Indeed, a few actually welcomed them whole-heartedly. "Advertising," avowed Jerry Della Femina, "is the only business in the world that takes on the lamed, the drunks, the potheads, and the weirdos. . . . Eccentrics are drawn to the business and welcomed into it. Your best grade of eccentric is normally found on the creative side. . . . "[27]

Rather quickly, however, the romance began to fade. Not only did the equation of Creativity with eccentricity prove less than totally reliable, but many of the institutional hippies brought with them an arrogant disdain for both their more conservative superiors and the technical apparatus of the profession—a combination of ingredients which often drove their colleagues to a fervent wishing-them-gone. Unfortunately, when the hippies left an agency, they often took an account or two with them, and new agencies began sprouting by the dozens. "The structure of these agencies," sneered *Advertising Age,* "is so simple as to be almost absurd. . . . Just get an art director and a writer, add a tablespoon of marketing talent, mix it well, and the dish is ready to serve."[28] To an outsider, the hippies—and the more conventional but nonetheless counter-culture oriented colleagues they sometimes influenced—might seem an exemplary case of American ambition and verve. To the industry, however, both their creations and their ethics meant something far more destructive than admirable.

At the start, it was generally supposed that such stripped-down creative "hot shops," or even new-style creative enclaves within established agencies, could work advertising miracles. Unencumbered by either bureaucratic ossification or the presence of staid, middle-aged non-producers, the kids could communicate their way to instant prosperity. Within a year or two, however, people started wondering just what the kids were really turning out. "A good many companies," cautioned Dun's Review in 1967, "in fact are beginning to suspect that today's far-out advertising may be entertaining the public more but selling it less."[29] Within the industry also, suspicion and resentment began to grow. "There is no place in advertising for creativity that is sheer rebellion," asserted one executive at the undeniably creative Tinker agency.[30] And David Ogilvy, himself no creative parvenu, denounced the whole phenomenon in uncharacteristically scathing prose:

> The campaigns that I produced . . . included an extremely strong element of salesmanship. The new breed has no regard for how well an ad sells the product. These pseudo-intellectuals, these callow, half-baked, overpaid young men and women haven't the slightest interest in how the consuming public reacts to stimuli . . . . They are departing from tested formulae and going on to things that are very doubtful.[31]

Undoubtedly, some did. At its best, counter-culture-oriented advertising simply nodded toward the trends. At its worst, it verged on the preposterous. More troublesome than counter-cultural excess was a new emphasis on shock value, especially that associated with nudity. Of course advertising had long employed sex appeal as one of its heaviest-duty weapons. But, prior to the 1960s, the use of sexuality had tended more toward the ludicrous than the prurient: vapid cheesecake, inappropriate tie-ins to asexual products, and double-entendres of the not-quite-adolescent variety. But beginning around 1967, the new breed experimented avidly with nudity, explicit tie-ins, and near salacious innuendo. "Is there a difference," wondered The New York Times, "between 'Does she . . . or doesn't she?' and 'Had any lately?' " (the theme of a Chateau Martin wine commercial).[32] Probably, the venerable newspaper concluded. A bit more certain of his judgement, the irrepressible Ernest Dichter went into print with the claim that "many advertisers simply do not know how to handle modern sex appeals. . . . They are, in fact, old-fashioned about sex and how to use it in their commercials." By way of guidance, the discoverer of asparagus' hidden meanings offered the following:

1. Forget "puppy love" appeals.
2. Don't expect nudity and shock value to communicate sex appeal.
3. Look for new angles.
4. Why can't the housewife be sexier?
5. Look for more individuality in sex.

Finally, and as always, Dichter capped his advice with a bit of meta-speculation. In this case: "Sex isn't dying, it is simply changing. Smart advertisers will change with it."[33]

(Author's note: To paraphrase a certain famous after-shave commercial—"Thanks, we needed that.")

In sum, then, Phase Three of the Creative Revolution devolved into chaos, a condition tolerable only because of one crucial assumption: that there was a changing youth market to be exploited. One need not be sympathetic to the putative ideals and styles of the phenomenon in order to, as one analyst indelicately put it, "cash in on the cop-out."[34] As *Advertising Age* reported on one fortyish practitioner's primary research technique:

> Mr. Fladell's advice to anyone interested in selling to the contemporary market is to "take a 20-year-old, long-haired student to lunch. If you can finish your meal without getting sick to your stomach, you are half-way home toward understanding the huge contemporary market of today and the even greater market of tomorrow.[35]

But it didn't quite work out that way, either for the hippies or the advertisers. As early as 1967, a certain economic straitening could be felt. A year later, Norman C. Norman of NCK identified the cause. "More new agencies," he told *The Wall Street Journal*, "opened up last year than in the previous five years. . . . If Mary Wells is billing at a rate of $80 million after two years in business, some of the money had to come from other agencies."[36]

In an advertising agency, personnel costs normally account for about two-thirds of operating expenses. With dozens of boutiques each siphoning away a few accounts, established agencies found themselves compelled to trim their payrolls, sometimes drastically. The recession at the decade's end further tightened the squeeze as national advertisers suddenly slashed their promotional expenditures. Advertising found itself, quite unexpectedly, in the midst of its worst downturn since the 1930s, and Creativity rather quickly became an expendable commodity. More in sorrow, but also with a certain understated relief, Jerry Della Femina announced the demise:

> Well, it's over, kiddies. The so-called creative revolution is dead. Kaput. A victim of the recession of 1970. . . . As for my part, my only regret is that I don't have enough hair to go out and get a crew cut.[37]

As proof of the demise, Della Femina offered this bit of industry news: that WRG had recently captured the Alka-Seltzer account from DDB (whence it had wandered after leaving Tinker) with a "Let's-get-sensible" approach.

But what Della Femina did not, and perhaps could not, mention was that, while Creativity might be dead, the trend in no way pointed back to basics. True, the 1970s saw a return to research-oriented, as opposed to purely "creative," advertising. But the research began to produce a kind of advertising never before seen in the United States, an approach perhaps best captured in a headline for an *American Home Magazine* ad which greeted the 1970s:

"The Shrinking American"[38]

THE MERCHANDISING
OF DESPAIR

A college student I know tells me that he can break off a
relationship with one girl, begin dating a new girl, and it
will seem a continuation, not a change. He can develop a
conversation with the first girl and continue it with the
second as if he were still speaking to the first. By the same
token, he performs a boyfriend role for them. He is just
like everybody else they have dated.

Tony Schwartz
The Responsive Chord

"Love power" is the ability to communicate concern and
understanding. Love has taken Wells, Rich, Greene a long
way in two years. It's the hardest sell of 1968–'69.

Mary Wells Lawrence
Quoted in Advertising Age

On February 11, 1977, an ad appeared in *The New York Times.*
This ad, the first of dozens, was for *Playboy Magazine.* Its headline—"Good news for American business. Those young men
who wouldn't sell out in 1967 are buying in in 1977." And its
theme—*The Playboy reader. His lust is for life.*[1]

This ad campaign, however, was not intended primarily to
encourage those, whose lust is for life to hurry out and pro-
cure the latest issue, or even to subscribe. Rather, it aimed to
reach those *New York Times*-perusing executives whose corporations dispose of multi-million–dollar promotional budgets,
and to convince them that *Playboy* was an advantageous
medium in which to advertise. Given this intent, the advertisement might have offered the kind of hard marketing data

on which corporate planners rely: x million males between the ages of eighteen and blank, spending y million dollars on whiskey, sports cars, travel, etc. Instead, the initial ad featured a certain Joel Silverman, stockbroker, who said of his life in the 1970s: "I wanted good things to happen to everybody, but me first."

Commenting on the growth of Mr. Silverman's generation, the advertisement noted with approval that:

> They were remarkable then, intense and totally committed even as teenagers. A generation that had an earlier awareness of what was going on around them than any generation in our history. And what's even more remarkable is that today, ten years later, they haven't lost one iota of that intensity. They've just totally redirected it. They've traded SDS for IBM . . . [2]

Subsequent ads (which occasionally also offered marketing data) developed the theme. Twelve days after the initial run, *Playboy* presented a certain Wilford Smith, cosmetics executive, beneath the banner statement: "Those young men you thought wouldn't fit in after they served in Vietnam are fitting in very well."[3] Recalling that the war had "just . . . faded away" (ellipsis in the original), *Playboy* went on to compare Mr. Smith's generation to their victorious forebears: "Yes, this generation is making its mark as few generations have done before. In all, we think it's the most vital, alive group of prospects American business has been blessed with since the post-World War II generation."[4]

From other ads:

Wallace Dawson, senior sales representative, Xerox, appearing beneath the announcement: "Good news for American business. Today's younger men are no longer committed to poverty," and avowing: "'I figure if I buy it, I'll find a way to pay for it. So I buy it.'"[5]

And a certain Ira B. Madris, vice president/associate creative director of an unnamed advertising agency, whose photo held the place of honor above "They wouldn't listen because they *had* listened. And heard it all before. Up through generations, what they saw as an endless trip of hypocrisy, falseness, and blurred values. What they were saying was, 'You listen. It's not going to be this way anymore!' And it hasn't been."[6] Beneath this paean to Baby Boom virtue, in bold face print, stood the notice: *Retired young rebels for hire.*[7]

And Howard Kirschenbaum, manufacturer's representative: "Today I'm honest enough to know when I'm buying something for the sake of status and when it's a value decision."[8]

And John Springer, architect: "When I read *Time* I'm thinking about the world. When I read *Playboy*, I'm thinking about me."[9]

And through it all, *Playboy*, counterpointing its marketing pitch with encomia to a generation, with sycophantic pandering to a generation entirely unaccustomed to anything less than superlatives.

And also with therapy for the new personality of the 1970s: the narcissist. What *Playboy* portrayed in its series was neither simple-minded pandering nor hedonism for hedonism's sake. Rather, *Playboy* keyed its marketing campaign to the offering of what Christopher Lasch has called "strategies of narcissistic survival" in a world of ever-diminishing possibilities.[10] What "identity" had been to the 1950s and 1960s, narcissism would be to the 1970s—the trendy malady, and the next advance in the use of psychologically and psychotherapeutically-based commercial manipulation. It took a few years to get started, but once it did, the therapeutic advertising of the "Me Decade" set new standards of sophistication . . . and emptiness.

As has been noted, *circa* 1969, the Creative Revolution came, in the words of one adman, "to a crashing denouement."[11] The reasons for this demise have already been discussed: simple economics, changing industry structure, personnel turbulence. Mass closings and layoffs decimated the more junior creative types, while account and marketing specialists enjoyed renewed influence. The catharsis proved both painful and necessary, and by 1973 *Business Week* could conclude that "the advertising business was a lot cleaner, leaner, and healthier for the experience."[12] And so it was, when judged against the standards of financial solvency, managerial acumen, and institutional stability. And, as corporate advertising budgets began to revive, the profession was well-prepared to accommodate them. But a vexing new question quickly arose—what to say, now that the go-go years had gone. Some opted for a back-to-basics approach. "I believe," wrote Jeremy Gury, a senior Ted Bates executive in 1970, that "advertising, after some years of fanciful irrelevancies, is about to enter the most brilliant creative period in its history . . . but it will based on the *reality of the product.*"[13]

He could not have been more wrong, and the next phase of therapeutic evolution would be based, not upon product realities, but upon the new techniques of "psychographics"— of segmenting markets according to the perceived emotional and psychological characteristics of the consumerate. What M.R. had been to the pre-Vietnam years, psychographic market segmentation—and its obsessive interest in "positioning"—would become to the 1970s: a highly-touted panacea. But where motivation research, and indeed ego psychology as a co-opted whole, had confronted a relatively stable cultural milieu, psychographics encountered a bewildering proliferation of new modalities: those 1960s/1970s burnouts and permutations which went under the generic name *life-style.* Even *Advertising Age* confessed its bewilderment in a 1973 editorial entitled, "From the Age of Affluence to the Age of Alternatives."[14] By alternatives, however, the paper didn't mean just different ways of life. Rather, as used here, the term also included diminution, substitution, retrenchment, and the problems attendant on living in a decade of stagflagation.

And thus developed the central marketing dilemma of the 1970s: how to sell to an economically troubled, culturally fragmented, socially complex nation at a time when the dominant trends seemed to be not much more than cynicism, narcissism, and short-range egomania.

The solution: a new form of therapeutic advertising, an astonishing juxtaposition of pathology and cure, which cut across more traditional demographic and socio-cultural divisions, and which, simultaneously, offered therapy and exalted the self that required such ministrations.

For lack of a better term, the advertising evolution of the Me Decade might be called "life-style/narcissism." It took a variety of forms, appealed to numerous psychographic market segments—everyone from swinging singles to golden agers— and operated most blatantly in advertising's two most lucrative specialties: packaged goods and so-called "big ticket" items.

The blandishments came on strong. An early example of such "Feeling Good about Myself" tactics appeared in *Advertising Age* in 1975. The ad began with the headline, *I love me,* concluded with, *I live my dreams today,* and, interestingly, neglected to identify either the advertiser or the specific product up for sale. The following year, however, *Psychology Today* was running remarkably similar ads.

As the decade dragged on, a rash of research confirmed the possibilities inherent in this new brand of therapeutic manipulation. A BBDO study announced: "That more Americans now unabashedly say, 'I love me,' is setting the stage for what can be a giant marketing revolution," and Compton Advertising reassured the trade that "Americans past the age of 50 feel as much a part of the so-called 'me generation' as those below the five–decade mark."[15] Soon Hertz was declaring itself "the place where winners rent." Polaroid was proclaiming that photography puts you "one step closer to what you're all about," and a greasy-spoon short-order cook was asserting in *The New York Times* that: "Every night at 6 o'clock, Roger Grimsby and Bill Beutel report to a very important audience. Me."

Although the basic appeal entailed a narcissism so explicit as to be almost pornographic, life-style advertising could also present a more complex mien. At one level, it attempted to mobilize economic decay as an inducement to consumption."Live today," exhorted Pan Am in 1974. "Tomorrow may cost more."[16] A few months later, in a somber "Right now is the time to buy a new car" encyclical, GM chairman R. C. Gerstenberg announced that not only would the price never be lower, but that the purchase of a new car was almost a patriotic duty (shades of the 1930s minus the Depression).[17] Nor had advertising any compunctions about appeals to less fortunate strata. Midway through the decade, A-1 Steak Sauce ran a campaign in which a sturdy, mildly-ethnic man in shirt sleeves waves his dinner fork at the camera, mutters something about having to cut back for a while, and then comments with approval that A-1 "makes every bite count." By 1980, though, the folks in the A-1 ads had cut back so drastically that they were no longer even pouring it on steak. One commercial featured a convivial gathering in which some one queries: "A-1 on hamburger?" and another issues a stentorian "My friends, what *is* hamburger? Chopped ham?"

In addition to blatant narcissism and exhortations to "live your life today," advertising also revivified an approach at least as old as salesmanship. In the 1970s, the profession sought to co-opt consumer cynicism itself, in a manner rather evocative of Decius in Shakespeare's *Julius Caesar:* "But when I tell him he hates flatterers, he says he does, being then most flattered." In its commercial adaptation, this tactic attempted to link skepticism and cynicism with merchandise, either by praising the consumer as one damnably tough customer (especially the female of the species), or else by mocking the commercial itself. In one magazine ad, for example, a hard-faced woman appears above the headline, "The last man I trusted was my first husband." In a radio commercial, actor Lloyd Bridges and an anonymous cold sufferer conducted a verbal *pas de deux* promoting Contac. At the end, the poor consumer gasped, "You're the guys on television," to which Mr. Bridges sneered back, "Yeah. We're the guys on television." Presumably, the impact of a celebrity exhibiting disdain for his medium and source of livelihood—and perhaps also for the naive consumer—would gratify the audience.

Beyond overt narcissism, stagflation-oriented appeals, and the cynicism approach, the therapeutic advertising of the 1970s also manipulated more traditional emotions. During the Me Decade, four general emotional appeals emerged. None of them was completely new; all rose to a new diffuse sophistication. Of these four, perhaps the most common was the merchandising of a sense of general aliveness, of a commoditized *élan vital.*

Now, appeals to aliveness had been employed long before the 1970s. But during the Me Decade they attained new levels of narcissistic emotiveness. And nowhere was this phenomenon more evident than in advertising for two types of not-exactly-life-sustaining products: cigarettes and alcoholic beverages.

For decades, tobacco advertising had portrayed the product as an indispensable adjunct to the "Good Life," as an element of self-expression, as a very fount of identity. Since most cigarettes are essentially alike, brand image has always been a crucial marketing device, and the 1970s witnessed an unusual array of offerings. From the traditionally virile Marlboro man to the new sado-masochistic Silva Thins connoisseur, from the cheerfully self-satisfied Virginia Slims young professional ("You've come a long way, baby") to the semi-unbuttoned female who glared down from the highway billboard and announced with arrogant belligerence that "Winston wasn't my first cigarette," cigarette advertising vended vitality and more. Such advertising, in fact, constituted what can only be called a kind of secular mythology. "By lighting a cigarette," suggests Raphael Patai, "[the smoker] is magically transported into the company of those 'superhuman' beings whose life is an uninterrupted sequel of excitement and enjoyment, and who are divinely endowed with beauty, eternal youth, health, strength, and supreme sexual attractiveness."[18] He might have added to his list of attributes, insufferable self-satisfaction.

In equal measure, alcoholic beverage advertising availed itself of appeals to life beyond the traditional invocations of conviviality and romance. Purveyors of beer especially, from the Schlitz "You only go around once so grab for the gusto" to Budweiser's "For all you do, this Bud's for you" to Michelob's "Where you're going you've always known it" (actually, an early 1980s entry). Interestingly, beer advertising would become more complex in the 1980s; for now, suffice it to note that it vended vitality along with its intoxicating and fattening properties.

And, of course, no survey of appeals to aliveness would be complete without mention of the soft drink industry. As a group, soft drinks offer little by way of tangible benefits. And yet, as Patai has pointed out, the ads "take a product that is, by and large, inocuous . . . and turn it into a Nectar."[19] To demonstrate the intensity of this effort to market soft drinks as Life Itself requires little more than a recital of, say, Coca-Cola's advertising themes. In the 1950s, Coke had offered itself as "The pause that refreshes," an unprovable though not unreasonable product claim. In the early 1960s, the drink moved beyond mere pauses to active participation in human events by asserting that "Things go better with Coca-Cola" and that, concomitantly, "Life is much more fun when you're refreshed." In the 1970s, however, Coke and its agency, McCann-Erickson, discarded these appeals in favor of fine-tuning an overt vitality authenticity approach—from "It's the real thing" (1969–1976) to "Coke adds life" (1976–1979) to the early 1980s "Have a Coke and a smile." (Dates here are approximate, since campaigns overlap and occasionally resurrect.)

But Coca-Cola in the 1970s held no monopoly on appeals to life. Not to be outdone, Pepsi went through a similar series of gyrations: from the 1960s "Pepsi Generation" and the perennial "You've got a lot to live" themes to the mid-decade's "Join the Pepsi people, feelin' free" to "Have a Pepsi day" (1976–1979) to the early 1980s "Catch the Pepsi spirit, drink it in, drink it in, drink it in."

Meanwhile, at the diet soft-drink level, a somewhat different set of therapies emerged. While "Feelin' free" was deemed sufficiently attuned to mass psychic needs, the poundage-conscious required something a bit more overt. Diet Pepsi obliged with the 1973 campaign slogan, "We've got your number— It's One," a reference both to the caloric content of the beverage and the consumer's life-style, ethos, and soul. In 1974, the motif intensified to a flat-out "You can do it," to be followed later in the decade by a more self-satisfied "You're drinking Diet Pepsi and it shows."

A few more examples before moving on. Mountain Dew's 1970s series: from "Put a little yahoo in your life" to "Hello, sunshine, hello, Mountain Dew" to "Reach for the sky, reach for Mountain Dew." On a more openly narcissistic note, the Canada Dry campaign in which tone-deaf stars such as Jimmy Connors sang "It's not too sweet" with unabashedly exhibitionistic self-satisfaction and RC Cola's 1972 paean: "If what you do is right for you, no matter what the others do, then RC Cola's right for you." As the decade grew more self-enraptured, so did RC, launching its "Me and my RC" refrain, an appeal replaced in 1980 by "You and me and my RC," thus adding a third significant other to a formerly dyadic relationship.

Which brings us to the second of the new emotional appeals: intimacy.

If vitality and the self-satisfactions attendant thereon found numerous uses in the 1970s, intimacy (sexual and non) received an even greater workout. To be sure, beverage ads had traditionally employed this theme, especially in the soda scenes of demographically-balanced composition, the endless on-the-beach volleyball games, etc. Beer ads also had traditionally vended a more macho sense of camaraderie. But in the 1970s, friendship and togetherness also found a number of other uses. "Good friends are for keeps," ran a 1974 AT&T ad. "Long-distance is the next best thing to being there"—an approach subsequently amended to the more evocative "Reach out and touch someone."

In the late 1960s and early 1970s, intimacy also emerged as a dominant theme for an institution hitherto not noted for its beneficent approachability: commercial banking. Here the slogans ran from an amiable "You have a friend at Chase Manhattan" to a Dichteresque "The bank that listens" to a suggestive "The bank you can get next to" to an even more explicit "The bank that says yes."[20] Commercial airlines also cashed in on togetherness in a number of campaigns featuring beatific baggage handlers, omnipotent ticket counter personnel, and flight crews whose personal (as well as professional) *raison d'être* appeared to be a total commitment to passenger gratification.

This is odd. A cliché among pilots describes flying as hours of boredom intermixed with moments of terror, and, whatever else bankers may be noted for, riant generosity is not among their professionally desirable attributes. Yet bank and airline ads veered away from what a rational customer might legitimately expect—competent financial services and reasonably comfortable and safe transportation—and entered the realm of therapy. According to the ads, one emerged from bank or aircraft having known a closeness to one's fellow men not experienced since Schiller penned his *Ode to Joy* and Beethoven worked up the accompaniment.

Moving beyond the intimacy appeals, but also linked to them, was the third new approach: an unprecedented use of the elderly in a variety of situations. For most of its history, advertising has all but ignored the over-sixty set (except, of course, for products designed specifically for them). As a rule, the elderly dispose of considerably less income than other groups, are comparatively less willing to experiment, and, given the American youth obsession, may actually alienate other groups of consumers by their presence in ads. But by the latter 1970s, the elderly had become astonishingly visible, appearing in everything from soda scenes to car rental spots to the long-standing duel between Folger Coffee's Mrs. Olsen and Maxwell House's Cora, both of whom spent their air time teaching the fine art of coffee-making (and, on occasion, husband-keeping) to the younger generation. At a somewhat less amusing level, one Bufferin ad featured an elderly woman slowly working her way down a darkened flight of stairs to the kitchen while a gentle female voice explains, "Mom's incredible. She still insists on making the family breakfast every morning, even when her arthritis is acting up." The moral of the tale is that other pain relievers used to upset her stomach, but she's managed to learn to take Bufferin. "Thank goodness she's more careful now," the daughter (daughter-in-law) gratefully concludes. In another ad, a TV spot for some sort of food (the exact brand now mercifully forgotten), the man at the head of the table expresses his satisfaction by suggesting, "You can come live with us, Mother."

Behind this unprecedented employment, or exploitation, of the elderly lay two rationales. First, the elderly were somehow "cute," an adorable mixture of benevolence and ineptitude—a theory that prompted *Advertising Age* to caution:

> Easy on "grandpa" ads. . . . Advertisers and agencies must become more sensitive than ever before to the importance of exhibiting solid respect and positive values as they work elderly performers into their commericials.[21]

Among these "positive values" were, obviously, family unity, tried-and-trueness, and a good cup of coffee every time. But when old people were used to reach the non-elderly, i.e., their children, the value evoked was often something other than unalloyed affection and care. It was, rather, a therapy for guilt—the guilt of abandonment, either physical or emotional; a guilt to be assuaged by picking up the phone more often, or by making sure that Mother takes only Bufferin. The problem of the physically and emotionally abandoned elderly did not, of course, originate in the 1970s. But Me Decade advertising gave an old sadness a new and ugly dimension.

These, then, were three of the four appeals which evolved into new forms of therapeutic advertising during the 1970s: vitality, intimacy, and the use of the elderly to evoke and assuage guilt among their children. But it was the fourth technique which, in the context of those years, seemed to exemplify the merchandising of despair. It was the invocation of a single word: America.

For generations prior to the 1970s, patriotic allusions had been standard advertising fare. They would return in the 1980s, albeit in a more sophisticated form. But the "America" tie-in of the Me Decade was not to love of country, or to respect, or even to any discernible creed. Rather, the intended image was that of one big happy family, united in a common love of merchandise and life-style . . . and the therapeutic effect of a mild reassurance that, after all the *Sturm und Drang* of the 1960s, normalcy had at last returned. A few examples of this tactic: Coca-Cola's "Look Up, America"; Seven-Up's "America is turning Seven-Up"; United Air Lines' "This land is your land"; and, of course, the classic "Merrill Lynch is bullish on America" campaign—a most impressive cattle stampede filmed on location in Mexico. Indeed, so pervasive had this type of advertising become that the *New Yorker* ran a little piece entitled "Patriotic Spot (60 sec.)":

> You're waking up, America. It's morning—and you're waking up to live life like you've never lived it before. Say hello to a whole new way of being awake, America. . . .
> We want what you want. It's that simple. And we're giving it to you. At work. At play. Because America works hard as it works and plays as hard as it plays. When America has nothing to do, it reaches for us. . . .
> We're Number One. You're Number One. You're a winner, America. And we know what you're thinking. We know how you feel. How do we know? Because we take the time to tell you. We take the time to care.[22]

A few weeks after this delightful parody appeared, American advertising took on a darker tone. It was the summer of 1980; the Iranian hostage crisis had become a national fixture. The item for sale was a new kind of car, produced by a corporation itself in despair. Chrysler was introducing its new, fuel-efficient automobiles via the commercial services of men such as Johnny Cash and Frank Sinatra. The spots opened with the spokesman staring full-face into the camera and pronouncing eight words: *"America's not going to be pushed around anymore."*

Buying a new car, apparently, would change all that.

THE STATE OF THE ART

Come the millennium, I think the greatest demand on the part of mass audiences is going to be for individuality.

Mary Wells Lawrence
Quoted in Advertising Age

Nothing is so common-place as the desire to be remarkable.

Oliver Wendell Holmes
The Autocrat of the Breakfast Table

Nothing could be easier than to summarize the advertising of the late 1970s and the 1980s. I can, to borrow John E. Kennedy's quip to Albert Lasker, give it to you in three words:

Something for everybody.

Precisely who that "everybody" might be will be considered in the next chapter. But for now, it might be useful just to sketch the current state of the advertising art.

As ever, the bulk of all advertising has remained relatively straightforward. U.S.P. and Brand Imagery have also continued to vend their wares. But there has also arisen, over the last ten years or so, a kind of neo-Creativity, this time mercifully devoid of the 1960s excesses. This neo-Creativity has produced some small, and large, delights. Perhaps the finest single commercial of the last decade has been a little gem for Coca-Cola, starring Mean Joe Greene, the (now-retired) Pittsburgh Steelers' football star, and a white boy about nine or ten years old. In this McCann-Erickson spot, the battered lineman, limping alone toward the locker room with the game still in progress, is offered a Coke by an adoring little boy. Greene first refuses, then accepts the bottle, drains it, and finally gives the boy his torn and soiled jersey. The boy beams back, and the commercial's therapeutic effect is undeniable. Writes one analyst, interspacing his words with those of the ad's creator, Scott Miller:

> "Undeniably, we feel good after seeing this thirty-second playlet. "A transition has taken place," Miller explains. . . . "The world is an unhappy place: your boss doesn't appreciate you, or your spouse, or your parents, or your kids." But in the miniworld of "Mean Joe and the Kid," "an emotional exchange occurs"—between adult and child, hero and audience, black and white. The black man still cares, with all the burdens he has had to bear. The kid can still dream of bright tomorrows, when he is a man and a hero. We can all still hope. We begin to feel good about ourselves and the world. Our hot button has been touched. And the medium of this human exchange, its symbol, is Coke."[1]

For once, the hyperbolic description of a commercial's effect is more or less apt. And, of course, practically no sentient American can be unaware of perhaps the finest example of sustained Creativity in advertising history: the Miller Lite Beer series.[2] This set of several dozen commercials, now part of American folk culture, was born in the 1970s, when Miller Brewing, and its parent corporation, Philip Morris, faced a fundamental dilemma. Beer consumption was declining, breweries were folding at an alarming rate, and light beer as a product seemed to have no future at all. The reason was obvious. The 20% of the beer-consuming market which accounted for 80% of total sales wanted the real thing, not some tasteless, watered-down concoction. Conversely, the calorie-conscious and the upscale, a rapidly growing group, tended to avoid the beverage altogether. Miller's promotional solution, a strategy handled first by McCann-Erickson, and then by Backer & Spielvogel, proved both unique and brilliantly successful. By using retired athletes in various stages of physical decompression (plus other luminaries such as comedian Rodney Dangerfield and writer Mickey Spillane) in humorous, mildly self-deprecating situations, Lite Beer enticed both the macho and the sophisticate markets.

The results were spectacular. Through endlessly amusing vignettes involving the Miller Lite All-Stars, Miller not only captured a major market share, but also came to dominate the public mind so thoroughly that competitors had to run defensive advertising. "Don't ask for just a light," exhorted Anheuser-Busch on behalf of its entry; "Ask for Bud Light." Not since the Avis-Hertz face-off had a major advertiser been forced to such "reactive" advertising. And, interestingly, the Miller Lite commercials seem to have gained almost universal public approbation, even among those indifferent or opposed to the product.

Other attempts at differentness, however, didn't fare quite so well. In 1980, (the year America stopped being pushed around) the consumerate reacted with unaccustomed vitriol against a new way of advertising an old product: denim jeans. In the context of the times, the pique seemed surprising. Or, perhaps, the ire represented an early warning of the kinds of cultural change which Ronald Reagan would find so beneficial later that year. In any event, the use of pre-pubescent models in explicitly sexual designer jeans advertising became a minor *cause célèbre.*

"He has winsome brown eyes," reported *The New York Times.* "She has tumbling blond curls, and neither of them is a day over 11 years old. 'You've got the look I want to know better,' he sings to her. Leaning toward him intently, she sings back, 'You've got the look that's all together.'"[3] This overtly erotic *pas de deux* for Jordache jeans provoked a truly astonishing, and apparently spontaneous, public and professional outcry, as did the slightly more adult (fifteen or so) cooings of Brooke Shields on behalf of Calvin Klein jeans:

> Smiling coyly at the camera as she hunkers down on the floor and spreads her denim-clad legs wider than the 21-in. television screen, the teen-age temptress murmurs huskily, "You know what comes between me and my Calvins? Nothing."[4]

Some of the ads were withdrawn. Others weren't, and, as Warren Hirsh, former president of Puritan Fashions, conceded: "We got a negative reaction. But I'll be frank; our business was quite good."[5]

Still another new departure bore out the adage that desperation can engender Creativity at least as effectively as genius. *Advertising Age* called the new *genre* "survival ads"— campaigns undertaken by major corporations to assert their determination to stay alive and in business.[6] After a series of well-publicized airplane crashes, McDonnell-Douglas ran ads offering encomia to their DC-10, and violating an axiom of public relations that one *never* calls attention to one's failures. Other corporations, emerging from lengthy strikes or damaging litigation, also mounted campaigns asserting that reports of their demise had been exaggerated. Often, such ads featured top corporate leadership, men such as former astronaut Frank Borman, who went on TV to announce that deregulation hadn't crippled his employer, Eastern Airlines, and that "We have to earn our wings everyday." Other senior executives, such as John DeButts of AT&T, addressed the consumerate on a variety of company-related issues. But, of all the "survival campaigns," by far the most famous and (as of this writing) most successful was undertaken by a company whose future seemed as dependent upon mass goodwill as upon technical and marketing expertise.

In his memoirs, Chrysler head Lee Iacocca reminisced on the dual problem confronting the nearly bankrupt corporation:

> We had to let people know two things—first, that we had absolutely no intention of going out of business, and second, that we were making the kinds of cars America really needed.
>
> Instead of our regular advertising, which featured pictures and text describing our new models, we ran a series of editorials expressing our point of view about the [requested Federal] loan guarantees as well as Chrysler's long-range plans. Instead of promoting our products, we were promoting the company and its future. We weren't getting our message across through the normal channels—it was time to advertise our cause instead of our cars. . . .
>
> The ad campaign was a major success. I'm pretty sure it played a role in the massive effort to convince Congress to approve the loan guarantees.

And there's no question that the ads had a real impact on the public.[7]

Iacocca had personally signed the print "aditorials." When the hands-on approach seemed to work, he was prevailed upon by Chrysler's agency, Kenyon & Eckert, to appear in television spots for the new, fuel-efficient K-cars. At first, Iacocca demurred, objecting that time spent before the cameras was time taken from more vital managerial duties. Finally, however, he consented, and appeared in a series of ads pitching slogans such as, "I'm not asking you to buy one of our cars on faith; I'm asking you to compare" and the now-famous "If you can find a better car, buy it." The advertising worked.

It worked, although not without a few side effects. When the M-1 tank, a Chrysler product, experienced performance difficulties, critics adapted the K-car slogan for Pentagon use . . . "If you can find a better tank . . ." (Chrysler ultimately sold its tank business to General Dynamics). And Iacocca himself was heard to lament that more people thought of him as an actor than as an executive. "It's a hell of a note," he concluded, "but I have a feeling I'm going to be remembered only for my TV commercials."[8]

Survival ads, along with neo-Creativity and a short-lived experiment with pre-pubescent erotica, all characterized the advertising of the latter Me Decade and the early 1980s. Lee Iacocca's brusque, macho honesty, Miller Lite's ex-jocks screaming *Tastes Great!* and *Less Filling!* with mock-menacing intent, and Brooke Shield's allures are still very much with us. But it was the therapeutic advertising of the 1970s which, in all its forms, has continued to provide the industry with its *leitmotif,* albeit in an ever more complex set of ways. So prevalent had therapeutic advertising become by the 1980s that it was nearly impossible to find a bank, supermarket, drug chain, auto repair business, or hardware store that didn't "care." Blatant humanitarianism and endless concern seemed a standard come-on, despite the inherent incredibility. "We do it all for you," avowed the McDonald's hamburger chain. "That," notes Michael Schudson, "of course is a lie. McDonald's does it all for McDonald's.'"[9] But caring, in the Me Decade and beyond, reached epidemic proportions.

At a somewhat more sophisticated level, paeans to self also continued to abound. Many of the more overt were directed at women.[10] Due both to rapid professional gains and the great divorce explosion, millions of women now found themselves in the market for products and services previously purchased by males: not just automobiles, but houses, insurance, brokerage, travel, etc. Rather rapidly, commercials now came to depict hard-as-nails female executives relaxing into near-orgasmic pleasure as they heard from their brokers, Superwoman business travellers swapping family photos with airline stewardesses, and, *de rigeur*, young females not only conversing knowledgeably with auto mechanics, but also driving Formula I racing machines—equipped, of course, with helmets which never seemed to disturb their hair-styles.

Of course, all this new independence also had its down side, and other therapeutic ads ministered to the walking wounded of the Sexual Revolution. In one sportswear ad, an affluent young man, clad in the manufacturer's slacks, prepares his apartment for what is obviously intended as a romantic evening *a deux*. He goes through the motions while chatting with an unseen interlocutor and, at the end, settles onto his couch, wine glass in hand. "What else do you need?" queries the announcer, leading the viewer to expect the instantaneous arrival of some young nubile. But it doesn't happen quite that way. "Nothing," replies the young bachelor happily. Fade out.

Two other motifs also saw increased usage. The "grandpa ads" of the Me Decade expanded into a series of promotions for items nor normally associated with the geriatric state. For years, AT&T had used old folks to tout long-distance calling. Now IBM employed a trio of park bench-sitting golden agers to offer a counterpoint of approval and acerbity concerning the computer purchases of local young businessmen. Wendy's Hamburgers ran its "Where's the beef?" campaign, made famous by Walter Mondale when adapted for anti-Gary Hart use in the 1984 campaign. Another corporate oldster, chicken

magnate Frank Perdue, took a good-natured swipe at both
Hart and Mondale. Appearing in a newspaper ad, holding up
a drumstick he asked, "Who cares where the beef is?" And, of
course, no catalogue of "grandpa" ads would be complete
without the two front-porch Bartels & Jaymes wine cooler
advocates, thanking people for their "support" at the end of
each whimsical message.

Just as the use of the elderly remained an advertising staple, so did the "America" tie-in, although in a more overtly
chauvinistic manner. "The pride is back," a Miller beer slogan, might adequately summarize all the campaigns for automobiles, beverages soft and not-so, and indeed a survival campaign for the American textile industry—"Made in the U.S.A.,
you better believe it matters to me."

Interestingly, the mid–1980s also produced a curious spin-
off: ads mocking the national competition. Both Miller and
Meister Brau employed Soviet caricatures. In the former campaign, *emigré* comedian Yakov Smirnoff noted that "In America you can always find a party. In Russia, party always find
you." In the latter, Comrade Petrinko, having absconded with
the money he saved by purchasing "capitalist beer that only
tastes expensive," seeks "big American car with tailfins."[11] In
ads emphasizing "freedom of choice," both Wendy's hamburgers and MCI portrayed Soviet society as rigidly drab and
endlessly frustrating. Wendy's put on a Soviet fashion show in
which all the models, dowdy peasant types, appeared in the
same ungainly outfit, while MCI portrayed a disheartened
Soviet consumer in search of meat. "No meat. Fish," says the
faceless counter clerk, handing him a fish. After two repeti-
tions, the disgruntled man returns with the complaint, "Fish
no good." To which the imperious fishmonger replies, "No
refund. Exchange" and hands him the largest fish of all.

Perhaps the anti-Soviet parodies were a legitimate reflec-
tion of a new American ebullience. Perhaps not. In either
case, though, it is fascinating to note that probably the longest-running therapeutic campaign of the era involved not a
product, nor even a service, but rather the *sine qua non* of
national existence.

Today's Army wants to join you. Join the people who've joined the Army. Serve your country while you serve yourself. The Army's willing to wait for you. A happy soldier's worth waiting for. There's so much more inside of you than anybody knows.

These slogans represent a policy at once ludicrous and disgraceful. They belong to part of an historically unprecedented experiment, an attempt, now nearly fifteen years old, to recruit a globally-committed military by pandering to self-obsession and relying on therapeutic technique. No nation in history, certainly no nation with global responsibilities, has ever attempted such a task. Nor has it been proven that the attempt has been a success, despite all the optimistic press releases.

In a sense, military advertising sells a product: military service as career, as adventure, as both. Recruiting advertising might also be expected to express certain values relating to one's nation and to the profession of arms. Prior to the 1970s, such advertising was generally undertaken by the Advertising Council as a public service. These ads portrayed military life in a more or less standardized fashion—as a blend of patriotism, excitement, and macho camaraderie. In strict legal terms, these ads might be considered guilty of misrepresenting the product. Before Vietnam, however, nobody cared to press the point, and indeed, the wiles of the recruiter provided a small bit of American folklore. But as the Vietnam War wound down, and as the Republic prepared to suspend its powers of conscription, the armed forces found themselves not only compelled, not only to attract volunteers by non-coercive means, but also to combat the era's pervasive anti-military prejudice. So, for the first time, the armed services, with the Army foremost among them, became paying advertisers on a large scale. And, of course, it seemed only logical to create the new advertising in accordance with the trends of the times.

Throughout the 1970s, it failed. The Army, in its first major campaign, all but promised potential combat arms enlistees a paid vacation in Europe, at a time when draftees were still dying in Southeast Asia. The ads aroused profound misgivings, both professional and civic. Commented *Advertising Age* as the Army pondered what to do next:

> If the U.S. Army decides to resume its recruiting advertising, we hope there will be no repetition of the ads which promise a young man 18 months of easy duty in Europe . . .
>
> When the chiefs of staff [*sic*] of the U.S. Army approved this campaign, where were their mental processes? . . .
>
> The promise of an easy 18-month tour in Europe denigrates the U.S. Army at home and in the eyes of a potential enemy . . .[12]

But if the vacation campaign (and its implied promise that volunteers would not be sent to Vietnam) both violated common sense and degraded the Army, the next major theme of the 1970s—*Today's Army Wants to Join You*—placed recruitment advertising at the forefront of the narcissistic/therapeutic *avant-garde*. The officer corps shuddered, Madison Avenue winced, and, had army life been a privately-vended commodity, the Federal Trade Commission might well have been moved to enjoin such ads. And again, *Advertising Age* demurred:

> To make an Army ad sound as if basic training is another Woodstock festival is as wrong as it is to give the Army a Spartan image [*sic?*]. To foster an image that blends discipline, adventure, personal growth and opportunity is something else again. We don't know the answer, but we do know that we'll be watching this campaign unfold. After all, we're the client on this one.[13]

The trade did watch, and at no time in the 1970s, the nadir (so far) of the All-Volunteer Force, did the Army's approach elicit praise. At one point, *Advertising Age* even suggested the need for an "ad corps" within the Pentagon, a unit that might at least shortstop the more flagrant gaucheries.[14] By 1979, one non-productive recruiting campaign after another, all based on distinctly unmilitary therapeutic appeals, plus the continued retention of the agency (N. W. Ayer) which churned out such nonsense, prompted a serious Pentagon review. As reported to the advertising world:

> The Pentagon has released a summation report by a private ad consultant and says the "all-volunteer Armed Forces are haunted by major 'product' problems that bigger ad budgets alone won't cure. . . .
> "If a similar situation were experienced in the private sector, it is quite possible advertising would be reduced until product improvements were made . . ." the report said.[15]

The Army's response was to launch a new, expensive, multi-media blitz. The new slogan: *Be All You Can Be.* Not a great soldier, or a stalwart patriot, just "all you can be"— whatever that might entail.

That the 1970s Army experiment with narcissistic/therapeutic advertising failed to meet either its recruitment or its image objectives need not surprise. What does astonish is that, even in the far more benign recruiting atmosphere of the 1980s, the campaign goes on. In 1976, a Comptroller General's report to Congress reaffirmed what every recruiter, and every adman, knows. Advertising works on people already predisposed to buy the product, and can neither miraculously increase the market nor produce instant attitude changes on the part of the general populace.[16] All the services compete for the same pool, attracting recruits by what might be termed a kind of marginal differentiation: uniforms, duty stations, mystique, training opportunities, etc. Further—a fact recognized both by *Advertising Age* and the other services—the young person likely to respond to a blatant narcissistic/therapeutic appeal is probably not the kind who should be avidly recruited. The Marine Corps, in a deliberate reaction to the Army campaign, ran a pride-and-discipline theme, looking for "a few good men" and promising no "rose gardens." What the Marine Corps did promise was to turn recruits into marines—a somewhat different U.S.P. than a vague "all you can be." So seriously did the Marine Corps take its own paid advertising that at one point an officer suggested that its agency (J. Walter Thompson) might profitably send the account group to boot camp for a while.[17]

For their part, the Navy and Air Force proved less rigidly traditional than the Marines, but also unwilling to follow the Army lead. These two services experimented with campaigns along more traditional lines: "It's Not Just a Job, It's an Adventure" (Navy) and "A Great Way of Life" (Air Force). And, in a 1980s departure, the services undertook joint advertising for the first time: "Army, Navy, Air Force, Marines . . . It's a Great Place to Start." An appeal to self-interest, to be sure, yet also dignified and not entirely unreasonable.

But again, the question arises: at whom were these ads directed? At one level, the answer is obvious. They were directed toward the eighteen-to-twenty-one year olds. But the eighteen to twenty-one year olds of the 1980s were no longer the products of the Baby Boom. This meant that, increasingly, the American consumerate was made up of three demographic segments: the Depression/World War II generation, now approaching retirement age, the Baby Boomers, and a new successor generation of youth.

And talking to these inter-related but nonetheless distinct groupings was becoming ever more complex.

VALS

Since they are motivated by growth motivation rather than by deficiency motivation, self-actualizing people are not dependent for their main satisfactions on the real world, on other people, or on culture.

Abraham H. Maslow
Motivation and Personality

Social distress and private unhappiness have coincided.

Herbert Hendin
The Age of Sensation

In the last chapter, I used two terms—positioning and psychographics—which now require a bit of explication. Both terms became *au courant* in the 1970s, although neither really represented anything new. The former reflected a new emphasis on the fundamental problem of American marketing: how to merchandise products and services that, in reality, differed little or not at all from the competition. The latter term referred to a new conceptualization of an activity at least a century old: psychologically-based manipulation. It is typical of advertising's history that neither of these concepts was recognized as an evolutionary product. But it is also clear that only in the context of the 1970s—the Creativity Burnout and the changing nature of a market in which human desires had outstripped economic realities—could positioning and psychographics have attained the prominence they did.

And it is also true that these two ideas provide a necessary conceptual link between therapeutic advertising as mere salesmanship and such advertising as public, and especially political, discourse.

Advertising is, obviously, not an activity undertaken in a

vacuum or *ex nihilo*. In fact, advertising forms only one part, and usually not the most important part, of what every business student knows as the "marketing mix."[1] In mnemonic form, this mix is called the "Four P's"—product, price, place, and promotion. The Four P's encapsulate the different aspects of marketing as a comprehensive business (or political) activity:

> *Product*—the physical commodity or service to be vended.
> *Price*—the dollar amount charged, either fixed or used as a basis for negotiation. Price may reflect no more than the costs of production and distribution, plus profit. However, price may also be used as a marketing tool to help establish brand identity. Most vodkas, for example, are essentially alike. Prices, however, vary considerably, depending upon whether the manufacturer wishes to attract an upscale or a lower-stratum market segment.
> *Place*—how and where the product or service is made available. Some commodities, such as Coke and Pepsi, are nearly universal in their distribution. Other products, such as women's clothing, are characterized as much by where they're sold as by intrinsic quality—boutique versus discount store, for example.
> *Promotion*—a complex of activities including everything from free samples and coupons to press releases to formal advertising.

According to the marketing texts, only when these four factors work in tandem does a business possess an effective marketing strategy.

But the term marketing is not synonymous with selling. In fact, many marketing experts view the two activities as antithetical. According to Theodore Levitt, an early (1950s/1960s) apostle of the "marketing mode":

> The difference between selling and marketing is more than semantic. Selling focuses on the needs of the seller, marketing on the needs of the buyer. Selling is preoccupied with the seller's need to convert his product or service into cash; marketing with the idea of satisfying the needs of the customer by means of the product or service and by the whole cluster of customer-getting value satisfactions associated with creating, delivering, and finally consuming it.[2]

In Levitt's formulation, selling starts with a pre-existent product or service, and asks only how to dispose of it. Marketing, on the other hand, begins by asking what the customer needs or wants (or can be induced to need or want), and then attempts to fulfill it.

Of course, when needs and wants can be induced and manipulated as well as merely discerned, the activity becomes more complex. Writing twenty years after his early advocacy, Levitt (now editor of the *Harvard Business Review*) suggested that the marketing mentality views any product or service as really four inter-related items, three of which are primarily mental constructs:

> The *generic product*—the unadorned existent.
> The *expected product*—i.e., the "customer's minimal expecta-
> tions."
> The *augmented product*—the technique of offering (or seeming to
> offer) the customer "more than he thinks he needs or has
> become accustomed to expect."
> The *potential product*—"everything potentially feasible to attract
> and hold customers."[3]

In Levitt's schema, the generic product must at least meet the customer's vision, the expected product. However, images of augmentation and potentiality are what hold onto business.

In a certain sense, this notion reflects little more than the traditional interplay of perception, blandishment, and R&D. But in the cluttered, complex, and stagflated marketplace of post-Vietnam America, a bit more was required. What was added was a practice which had hitherto been relegated to a minor status in marketing: placing a product in a particular stance *vis-à-vis* the competition, and doing so openly and aggressively. And thus was born, in the early 1970s, an obvious corollary to the marketing mode and a new progeny of the old U.S.P./*Brand Imagery* dialectic: positioning.

The "positioning concept" is both an advertising ploy and a form of hyper-aggressive marketing. According to the two admen who claim to have coined the term: " . . . positioning is not what you do to a product. Positioning is what you do to the mind of the prospect.''[4] A successful product must occupy a well-defined place in the market, according to its defining physical characteristics (if any). But it must, more importantly, occupy a definite place in the mind of the consumer. And, since positioning occurs primarily in the mind of the consumer, it is obviously essential that positioners know what's already in there, what there's room for, and where precisely it might fit.

And hence the conceptual basis of psychographics: the analysis and segmentation of markets, not only by demographic or traditional socio-economic categories, but also by psychological patterns and traits. Logically, positioning and psychographics can operate independently; they often do. But, beginning in the 1970s, the two in tandem became increasingly important generators of the research upon which most advertising, and especially therapeutic advertising, was based. And, by the late 1970s, many researchers had moved far beyond the simplistic usages of an Ernest Dichter (fountain pens are phallic symbols and don't forget the asparagus) to attempt the creation of comprehensive psychographic systems with a panoply of commercial and public uses.

Perhaps the best known, certainly one of the most evocative, of these systems is VALS. VALS stands for "Values and Life-Styles." A product of Stanford Research Institute (now SRI International), the concept received a certain publicity within the professional literature in the late 1970s and early 1980s, and general notice with the publication of *The Nine American Lifestyles* by Arnold Mitchell, VALS program Director, in 1983.[5] VALS represents nothing less than a comprehensive attempt at a national adult American typology, based on a 1980 survey of more than 1600 people, who were asked over 800 questions about everything from sexual mores to deodorant preferences to politics. VALS is significant for three things: 1) its premises, 2) its categories, and 3) the uses to which these categories, at least according to the author, may be put.

VALS is based on the premise that there exists a consistent, manipulable relationship between people's values, or what they claim to be their values, and their lifestyles. (A perennial question concerning the difference between "style" and "substance" will not be raised here.) According to Mitchell:

> [Values and lifestyles] tell us so much about who we are—as individuals, as citizens, as consumers, and as a nation. . . . People's values and lifestyles say a good deal about where they are going, and they help us explain such practical, diverse questions as: why we support some issues and oppose others . . . why some products attract us and others don't; why revolutions occur. . . .
>
> We started from the premise that an individual's array of inner values would create specific matching patterns of outer behavior—that is, of lifestyles. Neither values nor lifestyles alone, we thought, would be sufficient to provide the framework we were seeking. The idea was that behavior—private, economic, social, or political—is not random . . .
>
> We knew that, to be useful, the framework would have to be simple enough to understand easily and consist of elements vivid enough to identify with. This meant, among other things, that it could not have more than nine parts—a number selected because the human mind seems unable easily to retain more than this level of complexity.[6]

Now, the basic premises involved here, that human activity is neither random nor incoherent, seem reasonable enough. But something more is implied: a notion that, across the entire spectrum of human activities, the same motivations may predominate. And also implied is a sense of the basic sameness of these activities—that there may be no fundamental difference between what happens in private and in public, and why. This implied premise of sameness is the key to understanding VALS' significance, an importance which transcends even the inane theory that there can be only nine categories, nine "simple" and "vivid" categories, of adult Americans, and that these dominate all other goals, ideals, habits, and loyalties.

Inane . . . unless, of course, VALS' purpose is to provide marketers, politicians, and others with a useful manipulative tool.

According to VALS, Americans come in nine basic models, divided into four groups. Individuals may move from group to group in a variety of ways as they "grow" through the hierarchy. So too, at least according to Mitchell, may nations and the entire human race. But of primary concern here is not *homo sapiens,* just the modern American adult consumerate.

At the bottom of the VALS hierarchy lie the "Need Driven" types, specifically the "Survivors" (usually the elderly) and the "Sustainers" (recent immigrants, ghetto types, etc.). They constitute 11% of the adult population, or about 17,000,000 people. Survivors, VALS tells us, are "conservative" although also tending toward the Democratic Party, "mistrustful," set against sex between unmarried persons, and unwilling to see marijuana legalized. They also have few Master Cards or Visas, and their women tend to use less eye makeup, but more deodorant, than other lifestyles. Sustainers, who tend to be young, ill-educated, street-wise, and angry, transcend their basic mistrust and rage to the extent of carrying credit cards, eating frozen dinners, and favoring unmarried sexual relationships.

Next come 108,000,000 people or so, the "Outer-directed" model line. These are those who aspire to, or have attained, the "traditional" American lifestyle, as measured by family and materialistic values. They come in three models: "Belongers," "Emulators," and "Achievers." Belongers, the "Archie Bunkers" of the republic, are, of course, politically conservative (although often Democrat), regard their families as the center of their universes, and tend to own more home freezers, but fewer garbage disposals, than the national norm. Emulators, essentially ambitious younger people with odd ideas about what it takes to succeed, tend to be sexually permissive, keep small balances in their checking accounts, and avoid frozen vegetables. "Achievers," America's true old-fashioned success stories, tend to favor frozen vegetables, stable marriages and garbage disposals. "Achievers" are also skeptical of radical social change.

But if the "Outer-Directed" have traditionally been the source of America's success, their cultural dominance is being

challenged by a far smaller, but apparently much faster growing, model line, the "Inner-Directed." These folks, generally
Baby Boom types, currently number about 32,000,000, and
also come in three convenient models. The "I-Am-Me's," usually young adults who are still dependent upon their families,
tend not to read the business section of the newspaper, but do
like camping equipment and sex between unmarried people.
Frozen vegetables, disposals, and trust in the military score
less well. Economically, this group is hard to place, since many
of these self-obsessed young people report their parents'
income as their own.

"Experientials" are also quite into themselves, but older,
more settled, and economically prosperous. These 11,000,000
adults, who regard intensity and authenticity of personal experience as the true center of value (shades of Dr. Dichter), style
themselves as politically independent. They do, however,
simultaneously consume frozen dinners and worry about the
additives contained therein. They also avoid canned dog food
and brassieres; in fact, "Experiential" women wear fewer bras
(or bras less often) than any other segment of the nation.
"Experientials" also worry deeply about the depredations of
human beings on the environment and actively trade in various financial markets.

Above the "Experientials" are the "Societally-Conscious."
Over half consider themselves politically liberal; only 23 percent place much trust in generals and admirals. They also
drink more than the national norm, have plenty of money,
seem relatively unmotivated by it, and eschew dry cat food.

Finally, at the top of the VALS hierarchy, stand the "Integrated," those who have somehow managed to combine the
best of both "Inner" and "Outer Direction." Unfortunately,
since they constitute less than 2 percent of the total population, they do not yet form a definable market segment; VALS
offers no data on their preferences in commodities, issues, or
politicians.

And thus America according to VALS. And not just America. The British have no "I-Am-Me" segment, a conclusion
that might surprise a few hundred English rock stars and some

hundreds of thousands of their adherents. Germany lacks the "Societally-Conscious," an assertion which might come as a mild surprise to the Green Party. And, of the Swedes, 30 percent are "Belongers." Needless to say, Sweden, with its exemplary welfare state, has no "Survivors," at least in the economic sense. And beyond other nations, of course, lies humanity as a whole. Mitchell suggests that perhaps the future of the race depends upon its ability to negotiate the simple and vivid stages of the VALS hierarchy to a "truly integrated" lifestyle.

But VALS was not created simply as a sociological tinker toy, and Mitchell asserts that the system has a wide range of applications. The marketing and advertising uses are obvious, as are politics, because, as the author points out, "To get elected one must appeal to many lifestyles."[7] And, of course, VALS can also serve as a means of understanding others: employers, lovers, etc., and also perhaps as a further inducement to strive toward what Ernest Dichter might have called a "basic eternal summit"—a truly "integrated" lifestyle.

Or, perhaps, a melding of public and private, personal and political, marketing technique and ethical norm—a melding whose purest, most refined form is to be found in the ad.

PART FOUR

Res Publica

THE MARKETING OF CONSCIOUSNESS

> It is not only advertising which has become a tissue of contrivance and illusion. Rather, it is the whole world.
>
> *Daniel Boorstin*
> *The Image*

> Something has gone seriously wrong with everyone's images and models.
>
> *Robert Jay Lifton*
> *The Broken Connection*

At the beginning of this inquiry, I suggested that advertising comprises a system of discourse as well as a profession, an institution, and a purely economic activity. The contours of this system of discourse have, by now, become apparent: hypercompressed—indeed, almost instantaneous—psychologically-based persuasion and/or manipulation aimed at a low-involvement, normally inattentive audience. Further, for nearly a century now, advertising has also offered itself as therapy to the troubled, reassurance to the uncertain, and advice to the confused, i.e., to the vast majority of us (in one form or another). As adman Jerry Della Femina once put it: "Advertising deals in open sores. . . . Fear. Greed. Anger. Hostility. You name the dwarfs and we play on every one. We play on all the emotions and on all the problems . . . "[1]

Perennial emotions, true. The human soul remains ever constant. But advertising's therapeutic manipulations have not remained constant. Or, to phrase it a bit more precisely, the repertoire of manipulations has evolved in accordance with the changing interests and emphases of the psychological and psychotherapeutic sciences. From the relatively simple conundra of the early twentieth-century heart to more complex problems of identity and to narcissisms of varying persuasions, advertising has tracked with the scientific examiners of and ministers to the human psychic interior. Further, and of great importance here, the economic markets in which advertising operates have also grown more diffuse and intricate. Products and services are normally vended within the parameters of marketing systems, the array of real, potential, and imaginary satisfactions described by Theodore Levitt. Products and services must be positioned within that larger market, which means defined not only against the competition, but also within the minds of consumers. Increasingly, this process of positioning (and repositioning) relies upon psychographic market definition and segmentation. And finally, within the last few years, multi-purpose segmentation systems such as VALS have been devised: manipulative tools touted as equally valuable for the merchandising of products, or ideas, or candidates. While systems such as VALS may incorporate ideas and techniques other than the psychological, their manipulative/therapeutic applications are vast. In the world of VALS, every form of marketing is essentially the same, equally amenable to therapeutic manipulation.

It is necessary now to consider the entry of such activities into the public world, and their effects upon the discourse of that world.

Before proceeding, however, a small caveat might be appropriate. Advertising is speech. In a free society, free speech provides a *sine qua non* of existence; the concept of the "market place of ideas" runs deep in our history. And indeed, over the past few decades, American law has recognized advertising's evolving role in public discourse, accorded it limited protection under the First Amendment, and occasionally even encouraged its use. This alone represents a fundamental break with the past, and is as it should be.

For nearly a millennium, Anglo-Saxon common law regarded advertising as "mere commercial speech," subject to legal strictures in event of fraud, but otherwise deserving of no great regard. Common law notions of fraud, coupled with the doctrine of *caveat emptor* and the concept of the "reasonably prudent man" constituted the extent of the law's involvement. During late nineteenth and twentieth centuries, the United States moved toward more positive regulation of advertising, first as a means of preserving competition, and then for purposes of consumer protection. A number of regulatory agencies, most notably the Federal Trade Commission, and a formidable body of administrative law, were established. But as late as 1942, the Supreme Court, in *Valentine v. Chrestensen,* still deemed advertising an "inferior" form of speech, undeserving of First Amendment protection.[2]

In a subsequent series of decisions, however, the Court has virtually reversed itself. In the 1964 case, *New York Times Company v. Sullivan,* the Court distinguished between "commercial" and "editorial" advertisements, holding that the latter form, at least, merited Constitutional defense. Eleven years later, in *Bigelow v. Virginia,* the Court acknowledged that even commercial advertisements, when touching on controversial subjects, could be afforded protected status. In this case, a New York abortion clinic ran ads in a Virginia paper that violated two of that Commonwealth's laws, against abortion and against disseminating information about its availability. Noted Justice Blackmun:

> The central assumption made by the Supreme Court of Virginia [whose ruling the U.S. Supreme Court reversed] was that First Amendment guarantees of speech and press are inapplicable to paid advertisements. Our cases, however, clearly establish that speech is not stripped of First Amendment protection merely because it appears in that form.[3]

The following year, in *Virginia State Board of Pharmacy v. Virginia Citizens Consumer Council, Inc.,* the Court reaffirmed that "speech does not lose its First Amendment protection because money is spent to project it, as in a paid advertisement of one form or another."[4] In the same opinion, however, the Court noted that this freedom is never absolute, and that advertisements may still be regulated. Wrote Justice Blackmun:

> Untruthful speech, commercial or otherwise, has never been protected for its own sake. . . . The First Amendment, as we construe it today, does not prohibit the [s]tate from insuring that the stream of commercial information flow cleanly as well as freely.[5]

In 1986, in *Posadas de Puerto Rico Associates v. Tourism Company of Puerto Rico,* the Court seemed to backtrack a bit. In this case, a Puerto Rican casino business challenged a Puerto Rican statute forbidding them to advertise to Puerto Ricans, even though gambling was legal and advertising to tourists was legal. Justice Rehnquist, in his majority opinion, suggested that, since the state had the power to ban gambling, it also had the power to ban advertising, and that the ban was constitutional even though the advertising was truthful and the product advertised was legitimate. The implications of this reasoning have yet to be worked out.

American law, this case notwithstanding, has, by and large, conceded that the line between the purely commercial and the non-commercial—the political, the social, the spiritual—has been blurred. It is not my intention here to suggest that this decision is incorrect. Far from it. Advertising deserves protection as much as any other form of speech, be it Ciceronian rhetoric, obscenities with "redeeming social value," or the literature encountered on subway walls. Nor do I wish to propose that non-commercial advertising be subject to increased regulation. If the experience of the FTC in dealing with commercial advertising is any indicator, it can't be done—for the simple reason that, *in therapeutic advertising, traditional categories of truth and falsehood are usually irrelevant.* Rather, it is my purpose here to assess the entry of such advertising into the public world, and to sketch the parameters of

what can only be called "the marketing of consciousness"—
to assess, in short, a new and unprecedented form of *political
communication,* a form which the Founding Fathers might well
have judged abhorrent.

Now, the use of advertising as a technique of non-commercial communication is probably at least as old as the
Republic. Certainly, the World War I Committee on Public
Information provides a splendid example of the exuberant use
of such techniques. And, to be sure, the advertising profession
has always exhorted itself toward a certain kind of evangelism.
"Let's use advertising skills to make decency and integrity
fashionable," urged trade writer Sid Bernstein throughout the
latter 1950s. In a speech delivered before whatever groups
would have him, Mr. Bernstein, then the editorial director of
Advertising Age, exhorted his colleagues and their clients to

> . . . join with me in a project to make the *real America more like
> the pictures in the ads.* . . .
>
> We can try to make good citizenship fashionable.
>
> We can try to make it popular to be a good guy and unpop-
> ular to be a bad guy. . . .
>
> I think it is possible for us as advertising people to use the
> skills we have learned in advertising not to moralize—not to
> point out what's right (there are others far better qualified for
> this task than we)—but to make what's right popular—to make
> decency and integrity fashionable.[6] (italics added)

That an adman might wish to perfect America by making
it a real-life advertisement need not surprise; that a professional in a business universally regarded as unscrupulously
cynical might wish to lecture the Republic on why integrity
and decency should be "popular" might raise an eyebrow or
two. Still, it must be said, the advertising industry had been
attempting something along those lines for quite a few years:
an effort that might be termed the "rudimentary" form of the
marketing of consciousness.

The Advertising Council, a direct descendant of the War
Advertising Council of the 1940s, has produced and/or underwritten [asking in return only a tax write-off] numerous "pub-

lic service" campaigns. The Council's efforts, and those of its agency and corporate members, have been expended on a variety of causes: forest fires, pollution, drunk driving, gasoline conservation, Savings Bonds, etc. The various slogans have become part of the American folk heritage:

> Only YOU Can Prevent Forest Fires.
> Every Litter Bit Hurts.
> Take Stock in America. Buy Savings Bonds.
> Don't Be Fuelish.
> VD Is for Everybody.
> America. It Only Works As Well As We Do.

So have the various icons: Smokey the Bear, the American Indian crying at the white man's litter, Brooke Shields toweling her hair while complaining about people who smoke, etc. All seem inocuous, and often times commendable. But, as Stuart Ewen pointed out in *Captains of Consciousness,* such advertising can easily serve corporate interests by redefining problems. Pollution becomes stray soda cans and Big Mac wrappers, not giant industries spewing millions of tons of poisonous byproducts and ecologically unsound merchandise. The fuel crisis is an individual matter, to be solved by individual conservation, and not by reforming the nature of the American economy, or by invading the Persian Gulf. Deforestation and attendant soil erosion are the depredations of careless campers, not logging companies. VD, alcoholism, and even mental illness become individual, not social problems. (Author's note: One of my earliest childhood television memories concerns a public service announcement about "What to Do When MENTAL ILLNESS Strikes." As I recall, you see a doctor.) Somewhat disingenuously, three students of the Advertising Council complained:

> . . . those involved in the production of Council campaigns come from a very limited segment of American society, all being drawn from the communications, advertising, and business worlds. Nowhere, either in the Council itself, or among the people with whom it works in the communications and advertising

industries, can one find representatives of forces seeking to change the structure of the American economy and polity and to alleviate the problems with which the country is beset—not through mere cosmetic treatment of the symptoms, but through a basic restructuring and reorganization.[7]

Point well-taken. And, sometime in the 1960s, those men and women seeking fundamental changes, of whatever sort, began producing their own alternatives. Commented Hazel Henderson, in a speech delivered before the Association of National Advertisers:

> "A whole new breed of commercials are pushing their way into the air waves set aside for public service advertising. . . . Civic groups are besieging stations and the Advertising Council for all kinds of bewildering new causes, many of them highly controversial and sometimes at odds with the financial interests of the very corporations which sponsor programs which support the Ad Council . . ."[8]

Unfortunately, neither page space nor air time can be made infinitely expansible, and as the profession grew reluctant to donate its services on behalf of strange new ways, a new kind of consciousness advertising took form. Interest groups, pressure groups, and a myriad of organizations whose titles inevitably included the words "Citizens for/against," League/Union of," and, (of course) "Concerned" started buying ads themselves. Almost simultaneously, disaffected types within the profession (this being the apogee of Creativity) began bypassing the Ad Council to contribute their labors to pet causes. Though no one went quite as far as one John Ziegler, who founded an entire agency dedicated to consciousness advertising and who offered "How-To" seminars at the New School for Social Research, volunteer efforts soon became a badge of commitment and authenticity for many among the younger professionals.[9] Tastes in crusades, of course, varied. Within days of Robert Kennedy's assassination, five junior staffers at Chicago's North Advertising produced a series of impassioned gun control ads, running headlines such as

"Write Your Senator ... While You Still Have One" and "More and More People Are Buying Guns to Protect Themselves from More and More People Who Are Buying Guns."[10] John Ziegler sang the praises of condoms.

Vietnam, of course, drew its share. A group called Advertising People against the War turned out a series of print and television ads, which they then made available to groups desirous of sponsoring them. The purpose of the ads, however, was not to end the war by direct action. Rather, proclaimed Robert Colodzin, the group's leader: "We had to make opposition to the war respectable."[11] (As opposed to merely fashionable.) Presumably, advertising could achieve the desired effect. Some ads keyed on the evocative, including one—a recruiting poster parody—which showed a battered, bandaged Uncle Sam above the headline, "I Want Out." Others addressed the reader or viewer more somberly. In one example, ad people implored their colleagues, "Help Unsell the War." This ad, appearing in *Madison Avenue Magazine,* not only assumed that the war had been sold, but that "gutsy advertising" could both end the war and help the trade feel better about itself.

Drug abuse, naturally, also drew its share of commitment, as did racial equality, clean air, universal brotherhood, and love. But, interestingly, the most publicized, and most effective, consciousness campaign dealt with none of the political or social crises of the day. Instead, it centered upon a common item of daily consumption and was, in fact, part of a two-pronged offensive: an aggressive campaign against the product itself and upon the right of that product's manufacturers to advertise their wares. It was consciousness advertising of a uniquely hard-hitting sort, and it almost succeeded.

"In the sense," wrote Thomas Whiteside at the start of *Selling Death,* "that the product involved serves no valuable external function, is habituating to its consumers, and that the use of it carries undesirable consequences—the responsibility for which the manufacturers are heedless, the selling of cigarettes is symbolic of the mass merchandising of consumer products in this country."[12] Not only symbolic, but also a caricature, for in no other product line (not excluding soft drinks) does imagery and therapeutic ethos play so important a marketing role. Smokers are almost invariably portrayed as either young and glamorous or older but virile—in either case, both immortal and content. To say the least, this is rather odd, given tobacco's addictive, carcinogenic, and anti-social attributes.

The issue of the relationship between smoking and disease lies outside the scope of this inquiry. So do the efforts of recent years to ban smoking from the Republic, one set of places at a time—restaurants, airplanes, offices, etc. So do the tendentious issues concerning the relationship between the tobacco industry and the Federal government.[13] What matters here are certain aspects of the decision by anti-smoking groups, particularly attorney John Banzhaf's Action on Smoking and Health (ASH), to attack cigarette *advertising,* and the effects of the longest-running and most evocative consciousness campaign ever created: the American Cancer Society's anti-smoking crusade.

Although the first scientific study linking cancer to cigarette smoking appeared in 1939, full-scale public debate began only in 1953, with the publication of a *Reader's Digest* article entitled, "Cancer by the Carton." Eleven years later, in January 1964, the United States Surgeon General released the results of a comprehensive study which claimed definite correlations. That same month, the Federal Trade Commission announced the initiation of procedures intended to force cigarette manufacturers to print health warnings on their packages. Eighteen months of byzantine maneuvering within the Congress and the bureaucracy resulted in the Cigarette Labelling and Advertising Act of 1965, which mandated the package warning, but also forbade government restriction of advertising before July 1969. There matters stood until June 5, 1967, when the Federal Communications Commission (FCC), responding to a complaint by Banzhaf, ruled that its Fairness Doctrine, which required broadcasters to provide "reasonable opportunity for presentation of contrasting viewpoints" applied to cigarette advertising. Thus (although the FCC specifically stated that its ruling did not establish a general precedent) something new was added to American public discourse: the notion that "purely commercial speech" could elicit political reply.[14] And, for the first time, broadcasters were legally required to provide free air time for ads carrying a message attacking some of their best paying customers.

John Banzhaf was, however, a lawyer of limited means. To implement this new-found right required the services of the American Cancer Society, a group which welcomes the FCC ruling with delight. Since producing its first modest anti-smoking spot in 1960 (a little homily on good habits by basketball star Bob Cousy), the ACS had found few broadcasters willing to incur tobacco industry wrath by running such ads, paid or for free. Nor had the Advertising Council shown much interest in offending tobacco interests. Now, however, the ACS, relying almost entirely on volunteer actors, some of whom risked and incurred retaliatory blacklisting, and on production facilities donated by true believers, the ACS turned out a campaign of unparalleled dramatic power. In one commercial, a gunslinger preparing for a Wild West saloon shootout gradually falls into an incapacitating, tobacco-induced hacking fit. In another, a bride and groom leave their church while the sound track replays their wedding vows. They get into a car. The groom takes out a cigarette. The action freezes, and the voice-over abruptly stops with the words, *till death*, as *American Cancer Society* appears on the screen. And, in perhaps the most famous spot, actor Bill Talman (Perry Mason's long-time TV courtroom adversary), himself dying of lung cancer, pleads with the audience: "If you don't smoke, don't start. If you do, quit."[15]

While these images of death attempted to counter the impressions of eternal youthfulness, beauty or rugged machismo vended by commercial cigarette advertising, a number of regulatory bills were percolating on Capitol Hill. The result was the 1970 Public Health Cigarette Smoking Act, which banned all television cigarette advertising after January 1, 1971 and which also rendered nugatory the FCC decree mandating free air time for anti-smoking ads. The results of the ban soon became obvious. Cigarette manufacturers, relieved of the need to compete on television, saved millions in promotional costs, while tobacco consumption failed to decrease dramatically, and indeed, may actually be rising again.[16] But of greater interest than this windfall was the corporate response to the assault on cigarette advertising: a two-point argument which raised a pair of fascinating issues.

The first response involved the propriety—indeed, the constitutionality—of banning advertising for any legally salable produce. (The *Posada* case, with its curious reasoning may have confused rather than clarified the issue.) Anti-smoking forces, for their part, conceded the general principle, but argued that cigarette advertising constituted a unique situation, due to the hazards of the product. (Might the same argument be applied to advertising by, say, nuclear power interests, or Armed Forces recruiting?) In any event, tobacco interests found that the evolving Supreme Court interpretation of commercial advertising as protected speech could not be applied effectively in their case.

So the second response, an argument of undiluted irony: *Advertising should not be restricted, precisely because it doesn't work.* While the anti-smoking crusaders resurrected Vance Packard's imagery of the omnipotent traducers, other analysts emphasized the limitations of the craft. Professor Vernon Fryburger, chairman of Northwestern University's advertising department, paraded Madison Avenue's diffidence and *Angst* on Capitol Hill, telling the House Committee on Interstate and Foreign Commerce:

> "The power of advertising as a factor influencing human behavior is assumed to be greater than it is. It is assumed that advertising can create wants, manipulate motives, and exercise some kind of hidden persuasion . . .
>
> Advertising is more likely to succeed when it promises what people already want, when it seeks to modify existing attitudes slightly . . . the elimination or curtailment of cigarette advertising would probably:
>
> (a) have little or no effect on people who are predisposed to smoke anyway.
> (b) make cigarette smoking less desirable for some young people and more desirable for others."[17]

He turned out, of course, to be right. But the expansion of advertising from the vending of commodities to the presentation of protest could not be stopped by simple common sense. Indeed, over the past two decades, consciousness advertising has become a permanent fixture of American public life. Practically no significant issue, from "Star Wars" to AIDS, has escaped such presentation.

But even as advertising has become a medium for the expression of dissent, it has remained a corporate tool. And, corporate America has also found itself in the business of using advertising in order to protest.

CORPORATE PROTEST

The inherent worth of . . . speech in terms of its capacity for informing the public does not depend upon the identity of its source, whether corporation, association, union, or individual.

U.S. Supreme Court
First National Bank of Boston v. Bellotti

Is Anybody Listening?

Headline of Mobil Oil Advertorial

A corporation is a legal person. It also possesses, in many cases, a corporate personality, i.e., an image. Some corporations are perceived as fast-track and ruthless, others as sedate or stodgy; some are seen as efficient and progressive, or efficient and conservative. Not a few are viewed as verging on the cadaverous. To the extent that such images diverge from a firm's technical and economic realities, they incur varying costs and benefits. Among the cognoscenti, a less-than-beatific image may have only a minimal effect. An auto manufacturer, for example, may not care for the public image of his parts suppliers, but so long as they deliver the requisite items on time, at a reasonable price, and adhere to a consistent quality, so be it. However, among those wholly or partly ignorant of any corporation's or industry's real workings (which is nearly all of us nearly all the time), image can matter a great deal. It may, in fact, come to serve as a substitute for, or evasion of, hard knowledge, and the effort required to attain it. Not only can image have an impact upon retail sales, it can also exert an enormous, albeit usually diffuse, influence upon a corporation's or industry's dealings with the outside world: upon public and political relations.

For nearly a century now, American corporations and industries have found it expedient to present themselves in a favorable manner to those who may lack real expertise in their endeavors, but who nevertheless can affect them—customers, shareholders, the media, the government, real and potential adversaries, and the public at large. Means available for such favorable presentations have always included corporate philanthropy, glowing press releases, the providing of guided tours, guest speakers, etc. And, of course, advertising.

"The purpose of institutional advertising," writes George Flanagan, a former practitioner, "is to fulfill legitimate corporate needs *other* than the business of selling a product."[1] These needs might include enhanced personnel recruitment and/or retention, protection from (or continuation of) governmental regulation, neutralization of unfavorable information (true and false), acceptance of future plans, etc. Beyond specific goals, institutional advertising aims at the creation of a generalized reservoir of good will among "significant publics" and the public at large. Often, such advertising is undertaken by trade associations. Themes may vary, from assertions of indispensability ("America's Railroads. Who Needs Them? You Do") to campaigns by individual corporations stressing their, and sometimes their industry's, truly beneficent effects upon the economy, the ecology, or whatever. In either case, the role is a dual one: both to gain consent for their activities and policies, and to foster an image of "responsible corporate citizenship."

These goals are, of course, clearly self-interested. Apparently, they can also be attained. According to one BBDO study:

> A close correlation was established between knowledge of products and services and belief that the company "cares." Almost without exception, ratings were two to three times as high for the well-known firms on credibility, willingness to pay more for products, and investment merit. The report summarized:
>
> If customers think that a company cares about the public interest:
>
> 1. They are more likely to believe its statements on controversial subjects.

2. They think its products are of higher quality.
3. They are willing to pay more for its products.
4. They will buy new products from this company more readily than they would from other companies.
5. They think the company is a good investment.
6. The company's stock tends to suffer less decline in an adverse market.
7. The company tends to enjoy a higher price-earnings ratio.[2]

Perhaps. Studies conducted by organizations with an interest in proving the value of their offerings must be taken with a grain or two of salt (or salt substitute). But it is undeniable that, beginning in the late 1960s, corporate America moved beyond old-style institutional and image advertising and into therapeutics—in a big way.

Prior to the 1960s, corporations had generally justified their existence along more or less conventional lines: a useful product or service, jobs created, dividends paid out, communities improved by sponsorship of softball leagues, etc. But with the rise of consumerism, ecological activism, affirmative action, general skepticism, and the gradual emergence of what Irving Kristol has called the "adversary class"—well-educated, well-paid young men and women who make their livings regulating or trashing corporate America—mere kudos for a job well done no longer served. The obvious alternative: the kind of therapeutic advertising that could portray megabusinesses as socially and ecologically committed, or else as concatenations of "just plain folks." Weyerhauser, for example, began touting itself as the "Tree Growing Company." Other businesses began using their own employees (or actors portraying employees) to discourse upon their competence, commitment, and humanity. But by far the most common approach utilized the psychologically-oriented jargon of the era in combination with paeans to commitment. A few examples from a rather large file:

"We're Involved" (U.S. Steel)
"We Hear You" (AT&T)
"World Citizen" (Monsanto)
"The Best Ideas Are the Ideas that Help People" (ITT)

"Getting People Together" (Boeing)
"Men Helping Man" (General Electric)

And last, "We're Working to Keep Your Trust"—Texaco's proud affirmation that such trust predated their resolve to keep it.

Not surprisingly, such therapeutic evocations occasionally devolved into outright moralizing, a practice deplored by both steel-eyed Naderites and advertising analysts. "Don't pretend your motives are loftier than they really are," warned *Advertising Age* columnist William D. Tyler. As evidence, Tyler cited a Sylvania ad concerning the crime-reducing effects of street lighting:

> Naturally we wouldn't mind seeing our name up in street lights everywhere. But before being business men, we're citizens. And husbands. And fathers. So we'd welcome any improvement in street lighting. Even if it came from our competition.[3]

For Tyler, this verged on utter hypocrisy. For William F. Buckley, it appeared as theft, inasmuch as any corporation's legal duty is to maximize profits for it shareholders, not altruistically recommend the competition.[4] Sylvania however, was far from alone in its zeal to publicize its Good Samaritan side. Other ads routinely strained the limits of credulity. But in the world of therapeutic advertising, claims need be neither true nor even credible, just geared to producing the proper affective response.

Arising almost simultaneously with therapeutic image advertising was another phenomenon which, in fact, represents a remarkable step away from such manipulations. According to S. Prakash Sethi, advocacy advertising—the use of paid messages to express corporate opinion—has a number of functions which clearly differentiate it from mere therapeutics:

> The rationale for advocacy advertising falls into one or more of the following categories:
>
> 1. To counteract public hostility to corporate activities because of ignorance or misinformation.

2. To counter the spread of misleading information by the critics of business and to fill the need for greater explication of
   complex issues.
3. To foster the values of the free enterprise system.
4. To counteract inadequate access to and bias in the news
   media.[5]

Advocacy advertising, then, deals in specific issues. It may
tend toward the therapeutic, but it also relies heavily upon
presentation of fact—more heavily than most product advertising. This is true not only because such advertising is issue-
oriented, but also because it is almost impossible to broadcast
advocacy advertising. The major networks, claiming that such
ads might force them to provide free air time for opposing
groups under the FCC "Fairness Doctrine," routinely refuse to
accept such ads (even though the Reagan Administration no
longer enforces the doctrine). Print media, however, not only
accept "aditorials" or "advertorials," but the nature of the
medium is far more conducive to thought.

The practice of advocacy advertising is, to be sure, highly
controversial; only a handful of corporations do it on a regular
basis. Most refuse to join in, fearing gratuitous alienation of
customers, stockholders, or the media. But the practice has
grown considerably since the early 1970s. And nowhere has
advocacy advertising been more visible, and more controversial, than in the energy industry.

It is true that the energy industry has the right to address
the American people in defense of its own activities and on
matters of national energy policy. It is also true that much of
the knowledge required to conduct a rational discussion on
energy matters is esoteric. And it is also true that much of the
energy-related advertising since the first oil embargo of 1973
has been, in a broad sense, therapeutic. But there is also an
exception here: a long-term campaign undertaken by Mobil
Oil Corporation which, whatever that institution's interests,
has proven to be, as former Mobil CEO Rawleigh Warner
described it, "urbane in nature and at least as literate and read-
able as other material in that [the editorial/op-ed] part of the
paper."[6]

But first, the bad news.

The so-called "energy crisis" began in the fall of 1973, with the October War in the Mideast, followed by the OPEC embargo and subsequent price rises and gas lines. Months before the initial scare, nearly all the gasoline majors had either dropped or drastically curtailed product advertising. Simultaneously, most shifted to what is known as demarketing—advertising designed to *decrease* consumption.[7] The new ads both touted fuel conservation and adopted more or less overt Cassandra motifs concerning the impending era of permanent scarcity, a change openly acknowledged by *Advertising Age* as preparing the public for what still lay months ahead.[8] When the OPEC embargo struck, the oil majors loosed such a barrage of carefully prepared we-told-you-so's that both the FTC and Congress made noises to investigate.[9] Even *Advertising Age* attempted, albeit judiciously, to demur:

> The oil companies, now more than ever, need the support of the media, of Congress, and of the public. But by arguing that they are in no way to blame for the energy crisis, that the rest of us just don't understand the true situation, and then threatening to cut off the ad dollar flow, the oil companies are doing a lot to create a great big credibility gap of their own [10]

In the spring of 1974, when the energy crisis suddenly abated, energy advertising settled into siege warfare. "Institutional ad budgets," reported *Advertising Age* in 1980, "have not increased dramatically, but [oil company] corporate messages are now developed far more rapidly, almost in anticipation of the now predictable outcry that follows the announcement of hefty profit increases."[11] Such advertising included occasional lessons in the economics of oil (and, supposedly, of America), but also strayed back toward the emotional, and occasionally toward a thinly-veiled anti-Arab ethnic caricature. (An interesting approach for business so dependent on Arab good will.)

And yet, it is noteworthy that, while the most visible of the oil campaigns—and, indeed, the most visible advocacy program ever—clearly and unabashedly served the interests of its creator, Mobil, the ads also demonstrated an immense potential for the improvement of public discourse. Mobil advocacy advertising may not represent the wave of the future in a business dominated by image and therapeutics, but the campaign does merit at least brief attention here. One need not agree with the opinions in order to respect the product.

The Mobil "advertorial" campaign—the placing of ads on newspaper op-ed pages—began in 1970. The first ad, an attention-getter, dealt with the need for more mass transit. By 1973, though, Mobil was clearly using its op-ed space to prepare the public for the OPEC embargo. According to Herb Schmertz, Mobil Vice President for Public Relations:

> Owing to the nature of the oil business, our information from the Middle East tends to be fairly reliable. In 1973, we had the strong impression that tensions between Israel and the Arab world were close to the boiling point. . . .
>
> We thought it important to point out that America, too, had a stake in Middle East peace, if for no other reason than the prospect of a major disruption in our oil supplies in the event of war—a possibility that in our view was growing more likely every week. . . .[12]

Since then, Mobil has defended its interests aggressively and, by some accounts, successfully. Suggests Schmertz:

> When you're selling ideas, the results are especially hard to quantify. But it's clear that through our op-ed ads, we've managed to bring some of our views into the public consciousness. We have won a certain degree of credibility with various key publics, and have apparently convinced at least some of them that the oil industry is neither monolithic nor antedeluvian.[13]

Schmertz then goes on to list some of the benefits to Mobil from the advocacy campaigns: the chance to be heard as well as happier employees and stockholders, more trusting and contented customers, and an improved operating environment.

Now, the veracity of Mobil's self-defense, and of energy economics in general, lies outside the scope of this inquiry.

Suffice it to say that, as I write, the price of oil has plummeted, gasoline now sells below $1 a gallon in many localities, and the oil majors are running ads bemoaning their present distress and warning that the relief is only temporary. In fact, in Schmertz' book, *Good-bye to the Low Profile*, published in 1986, he speaks repeatedly of the "next oil crises."

More preparation?

In August 1986 OPEC did reach a tentative "accord" to curtail production and in December 1986, an agreement to raise prices. Whether the agreements will last is, at the moment, unknown. But in any event, as Schmertz points out in his guidelines for achieving a distinctive corporate personality: *Being loved is not your objective.*[14] Italics his.

ELECTING OUR KING

> In the hands of a media master, a political commercial can become a work of art—impressive, effective, enthralling, and, in afterthought, disturbing.
>
> *Larry Sabato*
> *The Rise of Political Consultants*

> Fables are suitable for addresses to popular assemblies, and they have one advantage—they are comparatively easy to invent.
>
> *Aristotle*
> *Rhetoric*

If the Mobil advocacy campaign has accomplished nothing else, it has demonstrated that paid advertising can be a lucid, rational factor in public discourse. Unfortunately, however, in another realm of public discourse—that pertaining to the selection and election of political candidates—advertising has moved in precisely the opposite direction. Since the 1950s, it has been a cliché of American politics that candidates are vended like soap; since the 1960s, it has been a cliché that campaigns have become not much more than media events. But, as we have seen, soap can be sold in many ways, and media events can take on many forms. Perhaps the real problem lies in neither the vending nor the events, but in the fact that, increasingly, both have been cast in therapeutic form.

A caveat here: In what follows, I will not suggest that advertising—therapeutic, hard-sell, or any other kind—now constitutes the decisive factor in electoral politics. Writing in

Packaging the Presidency, Kathleen Jamieson, a professor of communication, claimed:

> Political advertising is now the major means by which candidates for the presidency communicate their messages to voters. . . . Ads enable candidates to build name recognition, frame the questions they view as central to the election, and expose their temperaments, talents, and agendas for the future in a favorable light.[1]

Jamieson goes on to claim that, since more people see the ads than pay attention to network news, ads must therefore be more influential.

The conclusion is disingenuous. A presidential election is a multi-year—some say a permanent—affair; ads appear only occasionally. Further, most advertising, electoral or consumer, targets the committed or those who, by a slight nudge, might be brought aboard. Further still, no campaign advertising can withstand the disasters which the media can cause by widely disseminated candidate mistakes and misstatements, televised emotional outbursts, suddenly revealed pasts, etc. No advertisement, no matter how brilliant, could have saved, for example, Senators Muskie or Eagleton or have undone the gaffes of President Ford. None could have saved Jimmy Carter. In fact, it may be argued that, the less important the campaign, the greater influence advertising can exert. In state and local races, where media attention tends to be less intense, as well as in primary elections, advertising may indeed be crucial. In a presidential general election, too many other factors intervene.

And yet, it is the presidential *agon* which defines us as a political entity. There are, after all, only two nationally elected officials in the United States, and the selection process by which they are chosen has become a national obsession. The subject of electoral politics lies outside the range of this inquiry. But, before proceeding, it is necessary to discuss another cliché—the notion that American politics is now thoroughly dominated, not by ideologues or by party bosses, but by the "new breed" of consultants: hired guns offering "full-service" political campaigns, in which advertising is one of the most potent tools.

Political consultants matter, of course. But it is dangerous to ascribe to them either omniscience or omnipotence. For one thing, many of them find it professionally-profitable and career-enhancing to hype their own importance. As Larry Sabato has noted:

> Elections, and the choices voters make among candidates, are too complex and involve too many variables to be determined by a single element. In most elections, the new campaign techniques, and the consultants themselves, probably do not make the difference between winning and losing . . . But due in good measure to journalists' "hype" and consultants' own superb sense of self-promotion, the *perception* is that consultants and technology make all the difference in a greater percentage of elections than they likely do.[2]

Writing in *The New Republic,* Fred Barnes suggests that the power of consultants, and of their advertising, derives less from their putative infallibility than from expediency:

> It's partly fear that keeps consultants in demand, fear that your opponent will get a leg up. If one candidate hires a famous pollster or media consultant, the other candidates have to get expensive consultants of their own. In the end, the consultants nullify each other in most races. But the problem for a candidate is that he's got to hire consultants to achieve this.[3]

Further, argues Barnes:

> At the core of the myth of political consultants is the notion that they can elect presidents. Nothing could be further from the truth. Consultants actually have less influence on presidential races than any other. The higher the visibility of the race . . . the less impact consultants have. Consultants do best when voters have few sources of information. . . .[4]

In other words, in political marketing, as in product, there are inherent limits. And in politics, as in marketing, the greatest limit is that expressed by Jeff Greenfield about political advertising in his manual, *Playing to Win: "Do not offend reality."*[5] (Italics his.)

Sound, common-sense advice. After all, as the Madison Avenue cliché has it: "Nothing kills a bad product faster than good advertising." Unfortunately, however, it's not quite as simple as that. For, in the realm of therapeutic advertising, categories of truth and falsehood, credibility and dissonance, reality and fantasy, are not so much blurred as irrelevant. Therapeutic advertising does not require anyone to believe in the truth of what is being asserted, precisely because, in most cases, *nothing is being asserted at all.* All that is required—indeed, perhaps all that is desired—is a brief encounter, resulting in a mild, perhaps not even noticeable, affective change.

In this section then, I will not argue that electoral campaigning has become a form of entertainment; others have so claimed, and with considerable justification. Nor will I suggest that the advertising aspect of the "election show" exerts a preponderant, or even a consistently significant, influence, regardless of the millions spent or the big-name talent hired. Rather, I should only like to trace the rise of therapeutic advertising as the dominant form (negative advertising perhaps being a close second) of political advertising, and note the special problems created in public discourse by such manipulations. To do this, it will be necessary first to provide a brief sketch of the early uses of political advertising, and then to consider three specific presidential campaigns: those of 1968, 1976, and 1980. Richard Nixon was not, of course, the first to run a "media" campaign, but his 1968 effort did provide a prototype for what was to come. And, looking beyond the immense differences between Jimmy Carter and Ronald Reagan, one can perceive a certain sameness between the two, and argue that, in both cases, the therapeutic ethos preceded the advertising. Both men offered themselves to the electorate, albeit in very different ways and with very different results, as "therapeutic" Presidents.

Jimmy Carter and Ronald Reagan. The Presidents You Can Feel Good About. The Presidents Who Care.

The use of advertising in American politics probably goes

back at least as far as American politics: handbills, posters, pamphlets, etc. By the mid-nineteenth century, the gimmickry of image and sloganeering was well ensconced. But advertising proper first entered American politics in the early twentieth century, with a few forward-looking admen pressing their services on some surprisingly reluctant politicos. Among the advocates, of course, the redoubtable Bruce Barton. When not speculating on the administrative abilities of the second member of the Trinity, Barton found time for a political avocation which, at one point, even sent him to Congress. However, promotion, not office-holding, proved to be Barton's more notable contribution to American political life. As early as 1919, Barton was suggesting that candidates "needed to be 'humanized' in order to appeal to 'the great silent majority of Americans'"—those millions who purchased the packaged goods he praised.[6] In 1924, he told the Republicans that their campaign "should be geared to projecting Coolidge as a warm human being who would touch the emotions of the American people."[7] Because of (or, perhaps, in spite of) this benign advice, Mr. Coolidge went on to win himself a term.

Unfortunately for Barton, Herbert Hoover proved less amenable to such visionary schemes, and The Republican Party didn't gain another chance to project warmth and humanity until Dwight Eisenhower consented to an experiment with Rosser Reeves' U.S.P. philosophy. Reeves, for his part, offered more than proposals to pound "I Like Ike" into the national brain-box. In 1952, television was becoming a national fixture; Reeves had pioneered a media tactic that had proven both cheap and effective. Rather than sponsoring entire programs, as many advertisers were doing, Reeves purchased brief "spot" announcements between shows; in effect, he purchased large audiences for a fraction of the cost. The Eisenhower campaign agreed, and, ultimately, a trio of USP's were selected: Korea, Communism, and Corruption. As one analyst has described the selection process:

> The first of the three themes to be tested described General
> Eisenhower as "the man to bring fiscal responsibility to Wash-

> Eisenhower "would clean up the mess in Washington"; the
> third acclaimed Eisenhower as a "man of peace." The results
> overwhelmingly supported "Eisenhower, The Man of
> Peace. . . ."[8]

Eisenhower strategists, adopting the U.S.P. premise,
decided to turn the image into an unequivocal Unique Selling
Proposition (a claim that no one else can, or does make), in
this case, a claim to end the Korean War: *Eisenhower: The Man
Who Will Bring Us Peace.* The General, however

> took a quick look and surprised his advisers by reacting nega-
> tively. He told them that he could not guarantee to bring peace
> . . . It didn't take the committee long to make an adjustment . . .
> "Eisenhower, Man of Peace."[9]

With the selection of the other two themes, corruption in
high places and Communism (a sop to the McCarthy crowd),
the campaign was conceptually in place. The candidate then
filmed a series of short pronouncements for a spot series to be
entitled, "Eisenhower Answers the Nation." Next, as two analysts relate:

> Now that the Eisenhower answers were in the can, the
> questions had to be filmed. Reeves wanted a diverse group of
> people. The original plan had been to send camera crews all
> over the country, to tape a random sampling of Americans.
> Some one—his name is lost to history—hit upon a money-sav-
> ing idea that Reeves quickly embraced. On two afternoons Bates
> employees mingled with the tourists at New York's Radio City
> Music Hall. Those who looked like "everyday Americans" were
> asked to come to the studio. There they recited questions from
> cue cards.[10]

The questions and answers were then edited, mixed, and
matched, and the results were encounters such as:

Dark-haired woman: "The Democrats have made mistakes,
                      but aren't their intentions good?"

Eisenhower: "Well, if the driver of your school bus
                     runs into a truck, hits a lamppost, drives
                     into a ditch, you don't say his intentions
                     are good; you get a new bus driver."[11]

And thus the age of televised political advertising arrived.
While Adlai Stevenson (who never much cared for the
medium) alienated the electorate by pre-empting cherished
evening shows with sonorous disquisitions, provoking irate
audience quips such as *I Like Ike But I Love Lucy*, the Republicans
appended their spots to popular shows which they hadn't pre-
empted. The Republican campaign also made some half-hour
specials—media events emphasizing pageantry, with Eisenhower's speeches (unlike Stevenson's) serving as little more
than an excuse for the display of enraptured crowds.

In 1952, then, the Republicans launched the age of mass-
media political advertising. It probably made no difference;
Eisenhower, by all measurements among the best-known,
most-liked, and most-admired Americans, was simply unbeatable. This fact notwithstanding, such aggressive use of commercial techniques drew decidedly mixed reviews. No one,
least of all Madison Avenue, viewed the development with
unmitigated joy. Advertising's reluctance was not entirely
altruistic. Although politics could indeed provide Madison
Avenue with new manipulative opportunities, such activities
could prove extremely hazardous to agency health. In any
campaign, demand for the product is volatile; the selling season is relatively short compared to the amount of preparation
involved; in the season's final weeks, panic-induced strategy
changes and human exhaustion take a ponderous toll. Further, there is, considering the stakes involved, remarkably little money to be made (at least compared with product advertising) and, rather often, the losers neglect to pay their bills at
all. Other clients of alternative political persuasions may find
their agency's advocacies sufficiently offensive to take their
business elsewhere. And finally, political work—especially in
the 1950s—seemed to harm the advertising profession as a

whole. Noted *The New York Times* in November 1956, after a virtual replay of the 1952 campaign:

> Both sides of the political fence had help from advertising. . . .
> And each side attacked the other during the course of the cam-
> paign for using the assistance of advertising, which by implica-
> tion was branded as an unfair and possibly unethical tactic. So
> while Madison Avenue techniques were helpful, Madison Ave-
> nue itself lost prestige.[12]

Such techniques may have been helpful, but they made no difference in 1956. Eisenhower was again unbeatable, and the major evolutionary advance (if such it can be called) during this season was the Democratic introduction of televised negative ads—a series of spots entitled "How's that Again, General?" which purported to demonstrate that 1952 campaign promises hadn't been kept.

Nor did advertising seem to make much difference in 1960, an election in which, by all rights, it should have. Media in general, rather than just advertising, seem to have determined the outcome. Nixon's poor image in the first debate proved especially damaging, as did his general aversion to television. Kennedy's aggressive campaign style, coupled with Eisenhower's tepid endorsement of his vice president, were certainly more important than advertising. Whether more carefully-targeted advertising in a few key states might have swung the election is certainly possible. Conclusions, however, must remain academic.

In 1964, advertising played an essentially minimal role. Lyndon Johnson was unbeatable. Graced by the nimbus of his murdered predecessor, running against a man who seemed more interested in being right (in both senses of the word) than president, LBJ had a relatively simple task. But the 1964 campaign produced what must be judged the single most famous use of political advertising in American history.

The ad itself ran only once, on NBC's *Monday Night at the Movies*, September 7, 1964. This commercial, a DDB product made by free-lance media specialist Tony Schwartz, opened with a little girl picking petals off a flower and counting, *One, two, three* . . . A man's voice went into a countdown, *Ten, nine, eight* . . . At zero, the little girl disappeared into a mushroom cloud. Then the disembodied voice of Lyndon Johnson suggested that we must love each other or die, and the announcer concluded: "Vote for President Johnson on November 3. The stakes are too high for you to stay at home."

As Bill Moyers, a Johnson aide, later recounted:

> the White House switchboard "lit up with calls protesting it, and Johnson called me and said, 'Jesus Christ, what in the world happened?' and I said, 'You got your point across, that's what.' He thought a minute and said, 'Well, I guess we did.' So Johnson was very pleased with it."[13]

But what, precisely, was the point? It was certainly not to create an image of Barry Goldwater as a nuke-happy menace; the Senator was doing that successfully on his own. Perhaps it was meant to goad him into a rash rebuttal. If so, it failed, and for once Goldwater had the nation behind him when he retorted: "The homes of Americans are horrified, and the intelligence of Americans is insulted by weird television advertising by which the administration threatens the end of the world unless all-wise Lyndon is given the nation for his very own."[14] The Johnson campaign withdrew the ad, but later broadcast a similar spot, this one showing another little girl eating ice cream while a geiger counter ticked and a woman's voice discussed contamination of milk by atmospheric nuclear testing (a measure Senator Goldwater favored).

But again, the ads made no difference; the conclusion was foregone. Some years later, Tony Schwartz, the ad's creator (a distinction which, it should be noted, others have also claimed) offered an explanation and defense of the ad:

> Many people, especially the Republicans, shouted that the spot accused Senator Goldwater of being trigger happy. *But nowhere in the spot is Goldwater mentioned.* There is not even an indirect reference to Goldwater. . . . The commercial *evoked* a deep feel-

ing in many people that Goldwater might actually use nuclear weapons. This mistrust was not in the *Daisy* spot. It was in the people who viewed the commercial. . . . Commercials that attempt to *tell* the listener something are inherently not as effective as those that attach to something that is already in him.[15]

Four years later, however, what was "already in" people was a matter threatening (it seemed) to tear the Republic apart. The issues were clear. Vietnam—both the war itself and the passions and divisions it had loosed—and violence at home—a heritage of racial injustice, reactions to it, and a rising new black racism, and white reactions to that. But superimposed upon these issues were personalities and pasts: specifically, the personalities of Hubert Humphrey and Richard Nixon. Humphrey, perceived as both Lyndon Johnson's lackey and too mild to deal with the disarray; Nixon, perceived as stronger, but also untrustworthy and possibly unstable. And it was this confluence of volatile issues and damaged personalities which permitted—indeed, which mandated—the first of the truly therapeutic presidential campaigns. Most often, the 1968 Nixon effort is portrayed as the first really media-dominated campaign. In reality, what was new was an unprecedented integration of techniques and tactics, all co-ordinated to achieve a therapeutic effect.

"He is," wrote Garry Wills of Richard Nixon, "the least 'authentic' man alive. . . . he will try to be what people want."[16] But what was it that people wanted in 1968, the year when, as Godfrey Hodgson put it, "all the issues came together as One Big Issue."?[17] Not withdrawal from Vietnam—not yet, at any rate. Nor racial violence, whether black or white. Nor limitless tolerance of those whom Nixon would later refer to as "the bums who were burning the books." Rather, in 1968, it seemed that the One Big Issue was finding someone to (as Nixon noted in his campaign) "Bring Us Together." This he set out to provide, in a campaign which skillfully evaded both his past and the issues, concentrating instead on what Wills has called the "orchestration of resentments"—a tactic aimed, not at inflaming passions, but at treating them.[18] "It was," concluded Jules Witcover, "a strategy revolutionary in approach and scope, and masterful in execution."[19]

And the advertisement was its paradigm.

Precisely when Richard Nixon determined to take another run at the presidency remains a matter of conjecture. He certainly had a firm base. As senior partner in the Republican establishment, increasingly at home in its eastern wing, and as leader presumptive after the 1964 fiasco, he still commanded influence among the party faithful. His 1966 activities on behalf of various Republican candidates had provided him with a number of negotiable IOU's. But to translate party standing into nomination and election, he had to do two things: first, shed the pugnacious, devious loser image and, second, replace it. At a 1967 strategy session, a meeting oddly reminiscent of Gerard Lambert's Listerine colloquy, Nixon addressed the first dilemma. According to William Safire, a participant:

> "My biggest problem," Nixon concluded, "is 'Nixon can't win' . . . "
>
> We discussed ways to build "winability." I suggested the "inevitability" theme, recalling how other leaders moved inexorably back to power after a period in the wilderness. Nixon pondered that possibility and then warned: "You can't repackage Nixon with PR. Maybe that's ok with a new man, but not with me. I'm a known quantity."[20]

And yet, a "known quantity" was precisely what Nixon was not, in 1968 or any other year. In 1960, he had seemed both trite and undefinable, a jungle fighter of long and unsavory standing, yet also shy and insecure. In 1962 he had astonished the country with his bathos at the "final press conference" wherein he announced to the press that they "wouldn't have Nixon to kick around anymore." But by 1967 he seemed more relaxed, more mellow, at times almost complacent, even, at times, at peace. And yet, confessed *The New*

Republic's John Osborne (no Nixon lover), this very quality of
maturity troubled him most:

> I keep waiting for Mr. Nixon to show himself. . . . I know that
> I and my companions wait in vain. . . .
> We of the accompanying press, who flatter ourselves with
> the notion that we never grant to any candidate the degree of
> faith he demands, debate with boring and incessant fervor the
> question that Mr. Nixon himself posed to a bunch of high school
> students the other day. "Is there a new Nixon?" he asked. . . .
> "All I can say is, you've got to look at the man, you've got to
> answer the question yourself."[21]

Perhaps Mr. Osborne, and the rest of the country, might
not have found Mr. Nixon quite so mystifying, had they ever
read the works of Theodore Levitt, Ernest Dichter, *et al.*, or had
they read a 1967 campaign memo written by Ray Price and
published in *The Selling of the President 1968:* Joe McGinniss'
attempt to do for political advertising what Vance Packard had
done for the commercial variety.

> The passage of time; this has clearly worked in our favor.
> The sharp edge of memory has dulled, the image has mellowed;
> people don't maintain their passions forever. . . .
> The natural phenomenon of growth. This is where I think
> there's the most gold to be mined. People understand growth
> . . . they expect people to mellow as they mature. . . . *The great
> advantage of the growth idea is that it doesn't require a former Nixon-
> hater to admit that he was wrong in order to become a Nixon supporter
> now; he can* still cherish his prejudices of the past, he can still
> maintain his own sense of infallibility . . . *We have to be very clear
> on this point: that the response is to the image, not to the man* . . . It's
> not what's *there* that counts, it's what's projected—and, carrying
> it one step further, it's not what *he* projects but rather what the
> voter receives. It's not the man we have to change, but rather
> the *received impression.* And this impression often depends more
> on the medium and its use than it does on the candidate him-
> self.[21] (McGinniss' italics)

This is how it was done.

A political campaign, by definition, involves personal candidate contact with the electorate. Prior to the 1950s, such

contact had long been both expected and necessary; gone were the days of 1860, when Abraham Lincoln could quietly practice law while letting his supporters politic for him. But Nixon's 1968 campaign was designed to enable him to bypass this contact to the maximum extent possible. Rather than touring the country as he had in 1960, exhausting himself and giving the news media opportunity to catch and magnify his gaffes, there would be a centrally controlled campaign run by a specially assembled team. One carefully pre-planned live appearance each day—a classic "media event," staged for the purpose of being reported and timed to make the evening news—would suffice. For the press, there would be a steady diet of courtesy and fluff. The real work of reaching the electorate would be done by advertising (to the extent that the news media would allow it by acquiescing in the strategy). As Joe McGinniss, in his flawed but essential book, put it: "There would not have to be a 'new' Nixon. . . . Simply a new approach to television."[23] And so there was: so new, in fact, that the media failed to recognize it or react to it in time.

The goal of this new approach was clear: the presentation of Richard Nixon as an ordinary man sharing the common resentments and as a mature statesman—a presentation which could be manufactured by evading political discourse entirely.

At one level, Nixon's advertising differed only marginally from Eisenhower's. Both used spots and half-hour shows. In his shows, however, Nixon never spoke to crowds, as Eisenhower had done. Instead, he answered questions from panels chosen with all the randomness of a brain operation. These shows were broadcast only in the regions where they were made. In his spot commercials, however, Nixon adopted a completely new tactic. Where Eisenhower had answered simple questions with homey competence, Nixon's commercials manufactured the image of mature competence *by removing him entirely*. The spots themselves were spectacular examples of cinematic virtuosity, striking montages of scenes from Vietnam, Appalachia, the ghetto, etc., voiced-over with excerpts from the candidate's convention acceptance speech. Juxtaposing the voice with the scenes created an image of "stability plus dynamism."[24] According to Theodore H. White, by mixing and matching the half-hour programs and spots in accordance with needs established by computerized opinion research, "they could present snatches of Nixon . . . real but controlled; he would reach the nation by spots."[25] According to McGinniss:

> The words would become Muzak. . . . a technique through which Richard Nixon would seem to be contemporary, imaginative, involved—without having to say anything of substance.[26]

Examples of such efforts:

> Scene: Purple mountains/amber waves of grain.
> Voice: "America is great because her people are great."
> Scene: American soldier with *Love* on his helmet.
> Voice: "I pledge to you: we will have an honorable end to the war in Vietnam."
> Scene: Appalachia.
> Voice: "Did we come all the way for this?"[27]

These ads were made by the finest professionals available, men who prided themselves on their skill. But, in one dialogue, reported by McGinniss, the makers confessed their misgivings:

> "The problem we've had," said Jim Sage, "in most cases, is Nixon himself. He says such incredible pap. In fact, the radicalness of this approach is in the fact of creating an image without actually saying anything. The words are given meaning by the impressions created by the stills. . . . The most powerful man in the world. And he's going to be elected on what he didn't say."[28]

Eight years later, Gerald Ford, Nixon's unelected successor, lacking anything better to offer, attempted an overtly therapeutic campaign of his own. "I'm Feelin' Good about America" served as the theme.

But it was, of course, Jimmy Carter, the first man elected president on the basis of little other than his therapeutic properties, who played that game successfully in 1976.

As I write, it is eleven years since Jimmy Carter won the White House, an obscure former governor who offered the electorate mostly promises of honesty, faith and goodness as the antidote to all the world's problems. It is seven years since the American electorate, vexed beyond endurance by inflation, humiliation, self-righteous impotence, petty vindictiveness, and an administration perhaps best defined by T. S. Eliot's line, "decisions and revisions which a moment will reverse," expunged Jimmy Carter from public life. The Carter years, to be sure, witnessed a few accomplishments. But, I suspect, the final historical judgment will consist of one exasperated interrogative: *What on earth was he thinking of?* How could any man achieving the American Presidency have possibly been so inept?

Perhaps the answer lies, not in lack of intelligence or energy, or even in a certain spasmodic ruthlessness, but in the fact that *therapy was all that Jimmy Carter had to offer*. A creation of the therapeutic needs of the American people, he ultimately proved that therapy, when confronted by reality, must on occasion give way.

As Jules Witcover tells the story, the creation of "The President You Can Feel Good About" began in July 1971, when Dr. Peter Bourne, a friend and adviser of then-Governor Carter, asked "'Have you ever thought about running for President?' Carter replied: 'No, I haven't, but if I did, here's what I would do. . . . ''[29] Twelve months later, Carter attended the Democratic convention, angling briefly for the vice presidential nomination and coming away somewhat less than awe-inspired by the party heavies. A few days later, psychiatrist Bourne (who would ultimately resign from the Carter administration for drug-related problems) wrote a memo proposing that Carter soon decide whether or not to "make the national scene."[30] Among the items which the future White House drug adviser saw fit to emphasize: start writing articles, maybe even a book, and "begin developing extreme expertise in a number of key areas so that you can be a leading spokesman on them nationally. There are many possibilities . . . "[31] A bit more adroitly, Atlanta advertising executive Gerald Rafshoon (who would conduct Carter's 1976 and 1980 campaigns) suggested that: "The first phase of any Carter campaign should be to formulate a heavyweight program and project a heavyweight image."[32] And, in the long memorandum which proved to be one of the foundations of the 1976 campaign, Hamilton Jordan told Carter to "attempt to develop the image of a highly successful and concerned former Governor of Georgia and peanut farmer living in a small rural town, speaking out on the pertinent issues of the day." *En passant,* the future White House adviser also mentioned that Mr. Carter might begin reading *The New York Times* and *The Washington Post* every day.[33]

The first part of the 1972–1976 campaign required Carter to achieve some kind of national visibility without revealing ambitions which would have, at the time, seemed ludicrous. Between his initial decision to undertake what his advisers called a "national effort" and his early successes of 1976, came three years of unremitting hand-shaking, networking, and media-chasing . . . and also Watergate, the Nixon pardon, the fall of Saigon, and Edward Kennedy's withdrawal from the race. By 1976, by dint of pure effort and availability, Carter had successfully established himself as a plausible contender. The next problem involved positioning, both within the Democratic Party and nationally. In this he had a dual advantage. Since nobody knew very much about him, he could shape his image almost at will. And since the American people had grown wary of the standard assortment of political products, there was an open market.

If Carter's 1972–1975 strategy had been based on not much more than winsome peripatetics, the 1976 push relied on expertly applied advertising and marketing techniques. The product would be distributed through the primaries, early victories engendering subsequent attention from the media, which could then be used to generate more success. It worked.

And the reason it worked was that, despite all the normal tailoring of messages for different groups and regions, the basic product remained remarkably constant: a man with no past to hide—indeed, with no really relevant past at all—incessantly spouting the notion that the state should be as "good and honest and decent and truthful and competent and filled with love as are the American people."[34] As Jody Powell reminisced after the victory:

> I think people draw an artificial distinction between what's an issue and what's a non-issue. There was a tremendous yearning in the country this year for something of substance you could put some faith in.[35]

Two years later, Carter's adman, Gerald Rafshoon, who had returned to his Atlanta agency after the campaign, moved into the White House. When asked why, he responded: "I'm going to save the President's ass."[36] Commented one unnamed source:

> "The sad thing is that Rafshoon still thinks it's a communications problem. . . . It has never occurred to him that something basic may be missing in Carter's presidency—an understanding of the political system and a willingness to make it work."[37]

And *Advertising Age*, which had once named Rafshoon its Advertising Man of the Year, noted somberly:

> First, like any good marketer, he'll have to decide whether the problem is with the product or the marketing strategy. Not having adequately researched the problem ourselves, we are not in a position to say. But we hope that if it is the former, Mr. Rafshoon will remember that no ad agency does the client a favor by hiding the truth, or attempting to make up for the shortcomings of the product with a campaign which oversells its virtues.[38]

Perhaps Mr. Rafshoon heeded the advice; perhaps he had no choice in the matter. At any rate, the 1980 Carter campaign must stand as one of the most quixotic and, in its own way, ugly exercises in American political history. The man who had promised to be competent had proven himself the opposite. The man who had marketed himself as a compassionate Christian had displayed a petty vindictiveness which, although perhaps intended to motivate his followers (as in his threat to "whip Kennedy's ass" and his assertions that Reagan's election would cause another Civil War) instead alienated almost everybody. The man who had promised never to lie was now widely perceived as unable to distinguish between image and reality, and consequently between truth and falsehood. One devastating newspaper cartoon showed George Washington with the balloon "I cannot tell a lie," Richard Nixon with "I cannot tell the truth," and Jimmy Carter with "I cannot tell the difference." And finally, the man who had run against Washington and who had never made his peace with that city, now had to stand for re-election.

Rafshoon's strategy turned out to be an odd amalgam. At one level, he continued the old "humanizing" approach, running ads that characterized Carter as "Husband. Father. President" . . . and as little else. Simultaneously, he attempted to merchandise, not Carter himself, and certainly not Washington, but the Presidency. According to Diamond and Bates:

> Rafshoon says his main goal was to communicate what the Carter presidency was. "I don't think we could've done anything else." Thus the first Rafshoon spots were positive. Some showed Carter the President and emphasized the toughness of the job. . . . Others sought to strengthen Carter's image by showing him inspecting carriers and missiles. . . . Another Rafshoon spot concentrated on the toughness of the Presidency, concentrating on Carter's long hours. . . . [39]

But as the campaign wore on, and desperation increased, Rafshoon turned to negative advertising even more blatant than the anti-Goldwater ads of 1964. In one spot, for example, a woman confessed that Reagan as governor didn't bother her because "California wasn't about to declare war on anybody." (*Plus ça change* . . . the 1984 Mondale campaign featured bumper stickers asserting, *Reagan '84 . . . War '85.*)

In 1980, probably anybody could have beaten Jimmy Carter. The man who did, Ronald Reagan, has been characterized and condemned as the final triumph of image over reality in politics: an actor as president. Yet, might it not be suggested that Reagan, like Carter before him, represents less the triumph of show business than of the therapeutic ethos? Was not Reagan in 1980 another dose of therapy, this time from the conservative side, and has he not remained so? The man's personal popularity has consistently outstripped that of his programs and has survived disasters which might well have crippled another leader. Lebanon, the deficit, the current Iran-Contra affair, a plethora of minor gaffes and scandals: None seem to touch the man whose presidency seems almost coterminous with the "Pride is Back" jingles used to sell Chryslers and beer.

Of course, whether or not the "Reagan Revolution" will prove no more long-lasting than any other form of therapy, remains to be seen.

THE FTC

We have reason to believe advertising agencies have highly sophisticated information about such things as motivational appeals. We want to learn what we think they already know.

> Robert Pitofsky (Chief, Bureau of
> Consumer Protection, Federal
> Trade Commission)
> Quoted in Advertising Age

Advertising can sell a bad product once.

> First Principle of Advertising

In 1984, a few months before the election, a book entitled *The Duping of the American Voter* appeared.[1] The title clearly indicates the attitude of the author, Robert Spero, toward political advertising. In his first chapter, "The Arrogance and Danger of Political Advertising," Spero proposed to apply the truth-and-taste standards of NBC and the regulatory guidelines of the Federal government to electoral advertising. Spero next examined a selection of campaign ads from various campaigns, in each case concluding that, had the commercials promoted products instead of candidates, they would have been unacceptable. In the book's final chapter, "Breaking the Back of the Political Commercial," Spero proposed everything from shorter campaigns to abolition of the Electoral College. Significantly, and correctly, he placed no faith in Federal regulation of political advertising. Although he never made his reason explicit, he may well have understood why:

In the realm of therapeutic advertising, regulation is not only ineffective, but also irrelevant. For therapeutic advertising aims less at promoting the product, honestly or dishonestly, than it does at creating a manipulable sense of beneficial encounter, which then substitutes for or augments other forms of persuasion. Whether the ad promotes soap, or presidents, or abortion clinics, or Star Wars, the process is the same. And this process cannot be regulated by law.

Today, advertising is, for all practical purposes, protected speech under the First Amendment, subject to the common law of fraud and misrepresentation. But for decades now, the Federal Trade Commission has attempted—sometimes vigorously, sometimes much less so—to regulate not only advertising's claims, but also its effects. The arcana of administrative law lies outside the scope of this inquiry. But before beginning a discussion of the larger significance of advertising as discourse and governance, it might be useful to take a brief look at the Federal government's ongoing attempt to regulate advertising. For the history of this attempt reveals a fundamental fact: Advertising may well be a metaphor of our civilization, but the fault (to borrow from Shakespeare), lies not in our ads, but in ourselves. In order to "break the back" of political advertising, Robert Spero proposed fundamental changes in the American political system. In order to "break the back" of therapeutic advertising in general, fundamental cultural changes are also needed. And, in this matter, the old categories of "true" and "false" just get in the way, as the FTC experience well shows.

By law, the Federal Trade Commission exercises primary cognizance over advertising in interstate commerce. (Other agencies, such as the Federal Communications Commission, Food and Drug Administration, etc., wield analagous powers in their own specialized areas.) As enacted in 1914, the Federal Trade Commission Act, however, did *not* intend the agency to function as the government's primary regulator of advertising.[2] In the beginning, the FTC's purpose was to provide continuing enforcement of the Sherman Anti-Trust Act, a measure then with a quarter-century's ineffectuality behind it. Section 5 of the FTC Act empowered the Commission to deal with "unfair methods of competition," such methods being "hereby declared unlawful."[3] Exactly what constituted "unfair competition" Congress left rather vague, although clearly the intent of the law was to protect competitors from each other, not consumers from the system as a whole.

This situation more or less obtained until 1938, when the Wheeler-Lea Act amended Section 5 to read: "Unfair methods of competition in commerce, and unfair or deceptive acts, are hereby declared unlawful."[4] Again, Congress left the wording rather vague, but "unfair and deceptive acts" could clearly include advertising. Somewhat less clear—but at least arguable—was whether or not Congress intended to expand the FTC's purview from regulation on behalf of competition to regulation on behalf of the consumerate.

Prior to 1938, the FTC's concern with advertising had been marginal, at best. Between 1938 and 1970, a new pattern developed: recurring announcements of a new get-tough policy, a few well-publicized accusations, then litigation lasting years, as in the legendary Carter case—or, how it took sixteen years (1943–1959) to get the "Liver" out of "Carter's Little Liver Pills." Despite this general aversion to strenuous activity, however, the FTC did evolve both a standing procedure for dealing with "unfair and deceptive" advertising and also a general heuristic concerning the nature of such abuses.

The complexities of administrative law need not concern us here. Suffice it to say, FTC procedures were, and are, designed to keep most cases within agency purview and out of the courts. Rather often, an advertiser accused of malfeasance may simply sign a consent order, agreeing to stop the offending practice, but not admitting guilt or incurring penalty. This procedure made eminent sense, given both the costs of lengthy litigation and the rather unflattering conception of the American consumer that the FTC had developed—a conception which made the words "unfair" and "deceptive" all-purpose bureaucratic weapons.

As indicated above, the Wheeler-Lea Amendment did not define "unfair" and "deceptive" in any useful manner. Obviously, the words can have meaning only in relation to specific persons: unfair or deceptive to whom? Over the decades, the FTC adopted a test standard of intelligence considerably below that of the common law's "reasonably prudent man." In fact, as one student of the subject put it, a semi-moronic "wayfaring idiot" came to be regarded as the proper legal conception of the American:

> General stupidity is not the only attribute of the beneficiary of FTC policy. He also has a short attention span; he does not read all that is to be read but snatches general impressions. He signs things he has not read, has marginal eyesight, and is frightened by dunning letters when he has not paid his bills. Most of all, though, he is thoroughly avaricious.[5]

Thus, for an ad to be adjudged deceptive, it merely has to possess the potential to deceive the aforementioned idiot. And the key word here is *potential,* for, under the FTC canon, it need not be proven that an advertisement actually deceived anybody (idiot or otherwise), only that it has some capacity to do so. Further, deceptive potential is determined with no regard for the intent of the advertiser, or even the literal truth of the ad. Instead, "experts" assess deceptive potential by the ad's total context, content, possible ambiguities, and whatever implications might be derived therefrom.[6] Parenthetically, it might be noted that all commissioners of the FTC are deemed expert in all matters brought before them by virtue of their status as judges—a situation not without its ironies, as in the case of one retired commissioner, appearing before his former colleagues as a private attorney, who was asked to demonstrate proof of expertise regarding the matter at hand.

But such is the legal and administrative apparatus which the FTC brought to bear on therapeutic advertising.

In the 1950s, as a rule, bureaucratic lethargy prevailed. When, however, the FTC did sally forth, a number of industries felt its wrath. For example, the makers of fallout shelters were enjoined from, among other things, offering "claims of blanket protection."[7] The commission also conducted a seventeen-year skirmish with the Geritol folks, in an ultimately successful attempt to get them to remove the words *Tired Blood* from their commercial lexicon. Television came in for early and special scrutiny. Announcing in 1957 the result of a four-month study in which a battery of government attorneys spent their workdays watching the tube, an FTC spokesman pointed out:

> The script for a commercial may be perfectly harmless. But something often happens when it is dramatized for the television audience. The girl who recites the script may wink an eye. Or the announcer may raise an eyebrow. The gesture may add a meaning that wasn't in the script at all.[8]

If nothing else, this statement displayed a keen grasp of the obvious. Two years later, the FTC again announced that its personnel would monitor the tube, this time from November 15 to December 15. In accordance with standing procedures, a crackdown was prophesied. Unlike previous threats, however, something of the sort actually occurred. For among the items which caught the regulatory eye was a Ted Bates spot for Palmolive Rapid Shave.

And the age of nonsensical regulation had begun.

According to the Ted Bates ads, the aforementioned shaving cream had an unusual property: It could soften sandpaper sufficiently to administer a close shave. (One hesitates to say "close and comfortable," since, as far as we know, sandpaper doesn't feel much of anything.) Unfortunately for Bates, the sandpaper in the commercial wasn't sandpaper, but rather plexiglass sprinkled with loose grains of sand.

The FTC demurred.

In the production of commercials, certain things are, unfortunately, technically impossible. For example, whipped cream can't be photographed; it melts too quickly under the lights, and shaving cream is often substituted. This is known in the trade as a "mock-up," a practice rampant in the early years of television. Bates' defense against accusations of unfair and deceptive practices was that real sandpaper doesn't look sandpapery enough on television. For its part, the FTC countered with an expert investigation to determine precisely how many varieties of sandpaper existed (a lot), how many could be shaved with normal pressure after normal soaking (none), and—an exemplary instance of bureaucratic thoroughness— how many could be shaved with heavy pressure after extended soaking (a few). Bates counter-argued that the ad was never intended to convey the impression that Rapid Shave could really enable the sandpaper-owning shaver to groom his product (Why would anyone want to?), but was only intended as a dramatic device.

So enraged was the Ted Bates Agency that it even resorted to advertising, taking out a full-page ad in *The New York Times.* Addressed as an "open letter" to FTC Chairman Earl Kintner, the ad asked: "Is imaginative selling against the law?" and candidly conceded that:

> We know that people *don't* shave sandpaper any more than they write with pens under water, shave peaches, or string their wrist watches to the propellors of trans-Atlantic liners in order to find out if they are waterproof.[9]

The agency concluded by vowing to take this threat to its imaginative-selling rights all the way to the Supreme Court. It did, thus affording the Nine Wise Men an opportunity in 1965 to declare such mock-ups illegal. The majority opinion was written by Chief Justice Earl Warren; Justice John M. Harlan (who confessed to a personal preference for electric razors) led three blade-and-lather colleagues in the dissent.[10]

In advertising lore, the Rapid Shave case has attained the status of a minor Dreyfus Affair. And, like the Dreyfus Affair, the ripples of controversy and imputation spread ever wider. Within a few years, Madison Avenue began to sense that its previously annoying but tolerable relationship with the FTC was evolving into something else. For, by the latter 1960s, a horde of consumerist groups was sensing in the FTC new possibilities for what they called "consumer protection." The so-called *Nader Report* on the FTC (actually the handiwork of seven Ivy League students in search of a meaningful summer) appeared in 1969, excoriating the Commission for everything from its workaday ambience (that of an underutilized Southern county courthouse) to obsession with trivia to general incompetence to a strange reluctance to hire such sterling specimens of humanity as Ivy League law schools uniformly churned out.[11] Although the report could have benefited from a somewhat less self-righteous and hectoring style, it did make a few valid points, confirmed by a special American Bar Association inquiry conducted later that same year. This investigation, requested by President Nixon, surprised few observers by its findings, but astonished many by its language: proof that Naderite zealots held no monopoly on vitriol. Reported *The New York Times:*

> A study group of distinguished lawyers and economists reported to President Nixon today that the Federal Trade Commission wasted much of its time and money on "trivial matters"; that its staff is characterized by "incompetence," especially at the top; that it does less work now with more people than it did ten years ago, and that it should be changed or abolished.[12]

Among the report's major recommendations: a shift in the half-century-old regulatory emphasis, away from merely settling cases of improper advertising on a more-or-less random basis, and toward industry-wide prosecution on behalf of the perpetually aggrieved consumerate. Mr. Nixon responded by appointing Miles W. Kirkpatrick, former chairman of the ABA investigatory panel, to head the FTC. This appointment initiated a two-year torrent of activity designed to eliminate FTC incompetence, confront advertising's abuses at long last, and generally make the world a safer place in which to consume.

Precisely why Mr. Nixon allowed this exercise remains a matter of conjecture; one former Naderite has suggested that he intended to use the FTC as bait for consumerist votes in 1972, and then scuttle the whole project.[13] In point of fact, something rather similar did come to pass. The 1970–1973 period marked a kind of regulatory nirvana, a consumerist dream-come-true, in which the FTC embarked upon a "more creative use of its enforcement powers" and, *en passant,* dem-

the utter inability of the legal process—common law, regulatory, or inquisitional—to master the new, complex advertising forms.[14]

This assault in the early 1970s took three related forms. To a limited extent, all three grew out of previous FTC logic and relatively rational consumerist trends. The degree of "creative enforcement," however, exceeded anything imaginable in the pre-Naderite past. The first part of the attack focused on the informational aspects of advertising, the second and third parts on its psychological attributes. In other words, the FTC busied itself with both its traditional concerns of factual honesty and fraudulent intent, and also with the whole diffuse realm of psychological and psychotherapeutic effects upon consumers. By mid-decade, all three parts of the attack had acquired a penumbra of the ludicrous, and serve to this day as splendid reminders that the private sector possesses no monopoly of idiocy.

The first approach, advertising substantiation, arguably possessed a rational justification. If an advertiser makes a factual claim on behalf of his merchandise, he should be able to prove it. Accordingly, in December 1970, Ralph Nader petitioned the FTC to adopt a general rule barring product claims unless substantiating documentation was filed with the Commission beforehand, and subsequently made available for public scrutiny—a proposal which, if adopted *in toto*, would have left Washington buried under a few million tons of paper. But Mr. Nader held firm. Asserting that the sole legitimate function of advertising was to promote competition by conveying information (a somewhat dreary notion), Mr. Nader urged an enforced end to both false and misleading advertising claims.[15] Seven months later, the FTC did in fact adopt a similar program, although one that stopped well short of Mr. Nader's plans for arboreal genocide. No prior substantiation would be required across the board. Instead, the FTC began demanding proof of claims from various makers of automobiles, electric razors, air conditioners, and television sets. "Eventually," said Robert Pitofsky, head of the Commission's Bureau of Consumer Protection, "we will get out orders against every major industry."[16] Describing the measure as a "self-help" program, Pitofsky drew a clear line between legitimate sales puffery and unsubstantiated claims. "If some one says, 'tastes great,' we are not going to ask for substantiation. But if they say, 'stops three times as fast,' or 'costs half as much as all competitors in its class,' we are going to ask what they mean by 'class.'"[17] Commented Ralph Nader on this unprecedented, albeit still rational, expansion of FTC enforcement: "If it's a first step, it's an encouraging sign. If it's a full answer to our petition, it's inadequate."[18]

As originally envisioned by the FTC, the ad substantiation program had two objectives: deterrence of false and fraudulent claims and encouragement of honest informational advertising. The program failed on both counts, and never attained the scope Pitofsky had envisioned. The reason-why seems clear: a major disconnection with the White House. Within hours of the announcement of the program, White House communications chief Herbert Klein expressed serious reservations about the effort's long-term effects and constitutionality—a clear warning to the bureaucratic zealots not to push things too far.[19] But the program never could have achieved the envisioned results. So vast was the economy, so few the number of consumers willing to avail themselves of FTC documentation, and so limited the Commission's resources, that a Senate subcommittee could conclude a year later:

> [Ad substantiation] is not a satisfactory mechanism for supplying useful consumer information in a timely manner: the ads are chosen on a selective basis; the process is time-consuming and inevitably results in the airing of stale claims; finally, neither individual consumers nor the FTC have the technical capacity to evaluate the validity and relevance of much of the data.[20]

Nor did the program exert much deterrent effect, because the chances of any particular company's violations coming to the Commission's attention, let alone receiving bureaucratic come-uppance, were practically nil. Indeed, observed Richard

Posner, himself a former member of the ABA investigatory panel:

> It would seem, therefore, that the real purpose of the [substantiation] doctrine is to reduce the Commission's costs in prosecuting false-advertising cases by shifting the burden of proof from the Commission to the respondent.[21]

In fact, it might be argued that the most plausible effect of the substantiation program was the exact opposite of that intended—to drive advertisers away from the verifiable claim and toward more ethereal realms. To put it simply, the FTC's attempt to move advertising away from the psychological and psychotherapeutic may have actually intensified those claims. After all, . . . "Me and My RC" requires no more proof than "Less Filling!" and, given the ambience of the times, might actually have manipulated a bit more effectively.

If ad substantiation proved counter-productive, the next FTC gambit, counter-advertising, self-destructed entirely. This tactic, used successfully by John Banzhaf early in his anti-smoking crusade, had by 1971 begun to show a singular inefficacy in reducing mass nicotine addiction. But neither the accumulating data nor the FCC's explicit disavowal of Banzhaf's legal victory as a general precedent deterred the newly invigorated FTC. This time, however, a tandem of corporate and Federal forces prevented further expansion of the practice. Networks regularly declined to broadcast free commercials attacking their paying customers; the FCC held hearings that determined that the effects of counter-advertising could be neither predicted nor measured; and even the White House intervened, suggesting that Kirkpatrick's proposal for mandatory free broadcast spots to counter controversial ad claims "would probably die a quiet death."[22] And so it did, the Supreme Court holding quite sensibly in 1973 that there exists no constitutional right to media access, and the FCC reaffirming in 1974 its opposition to the use of the anti-smoking campaign as a precedent.[23] All in all, it seemed a fitting demise for a proposal which had threatened to open a Pandora's box of competing sanctimonies, and which ignored two indisputable finitudes—those of usable frequencies and daily broadcast time.

Thus twice stymied, the FTC embarked upon its third, and most quixotic, attempt to rehabilitate the mind of the consumerate. The new idea, corrective advertising, held that the FTC could compel an advertiser deemed guilty of deceptive practice to make amends by advertising against himself—a practice routinely employed in other forms of discourse, such as brainwashing, Stalinist show trials, and Marxist self-criticism sessions. Further, since the traditional standard of deception was psychological rather than factual, potential rather than real, therapeutic advertising could be attacked along with more traditional kinds.

With the evidence of psychological deception provided, of course, by the psychologists.[24]

The Commission's first foray into corrective advertising, however, did not engage the depths of the human psyche. Rather, the idea appeared during an otherwise uneventful action against an old demon—the mock-up. But while the Rapid Shave case had been primarily an in-house affair, the Campbell's Soup *cause célèbre* involved an outsider: John Banzhaf, formerly of ASH, who now mobilized SOUP (Students Opposed to Unfair Practices) in order to defend the consumerate against certain photographs of Campbell's vegetable soup which contained colorless marbles at the bottom of the bowl.

The tripartite combat began in September 1969, when the FTC announced a proposed consent order, enjoining Campbell and its agency (BBDO) from any further marble-izing, a practice they had abandoned a few months before. The FTC consent order had come in response to a complaint alleging that such a mock-up made the soup appear richer in vegetables and other life-giving nutrients than was actually the case. (Seven years later, the identity of the informer was revealed: H. J. Heinz. Campbell subsequently avenged itself by turning in

Heinz for excessive mold in its ketchup.) In typical fashion, Campbell and BBDO prepared to sign the consent order to stop a practice they had already ceased, while simultaneously denying any wrong-doing. According to *The Wall Street Journal:*

> Campbell said it "does not believe its advertising was ever misleading. No extra food ingredients have ever been added. . . . But since the ingredients naturally present have a tendency to sink to the bottom and be invisible in photographs, the ingredients were supported closer to the surface so they could be seen in a picture.[25]

Thus the situation: an impending settlement of a minor matter involving a discontinued practice probably required by the exigencies of commercial-filming. Then John Banzhaf stood up for all of us who had been tricked (for decades) into buying Campbell's soup over and over and over again.

In essence, what SOUP (a quintet of Banzhaf's George Washington University law students) desired was the right to participate in the case and the adoption of their proposed penalty: that Campbell be compelled to include in future promotions an announcement that previous photography had lied. Although SOUP self-confidently claimed the right to speak for the entire Republic (or, at least that portion of it that likes soup), the pre-Kirkpatrick FTC shied away from anything so drastic as compelling an advertiser to bellow *mea culpa* through the air waves and printed page. Two years later, however, the Commission, having shed its former reticence, adopted corrective advertising as its enforcement weapon of choice.

In truth, there had been such tendencies in government before SOUP bubbled over. The Food and Drug Administration, prime regulator of prescription drug advertising, had routinely employed this practice, although also admitting to Congress that "they don't know the effect, if any, of 'corrective' ads and other measures that they have taken to counteract misleading ads."[26] The FTC had also once dabbled with the idea. In 1964, midway through its Geritol crusade, the Commission had informed the J. B. Williams Company that if it intended to advertise Geritol as a specific for fatigue, it had to include an "affirmative disclosure" regarding the potion's rejuvenative limitations.[27] But not until 1971 did the FTC attempt anything as dramatic as ordering an advertiser to correct past and, according to the FTC, cumulating deceptions.

As already mentioned, the FTC, in its "marbles" ruling, had declined to order SOUP's desire: corrective advertising. It did, however, affirm its power to do so under the proper circumstances. In his first opinion as FTC Chairman, Caspar Weinberger (who subsequently found employment at the Pentagon) denied that "there is any disagreement between the Commission and petitioner [SOUP] as to the scope of the order which the Commission has the power to issue in this case."[28] But Weinberger questioned the efficacy of forcing Campbell to run ads in the 1970s atoning for deceptions of the 1960s and also doubted the gravity of the issue. "What principally persuades us," he wrote, " . . . is that the Commission has other important matters to deal with."[29]

SOUP, for its part, chose to disregard this rather unsubtle hint. Delighted with the theoretical concession, Aaron Handelman, chairman of the implacable vigilante group, announced: "Now the next step is to push them into doing it."[30]

Thirteen months later, the FTC did. This time, however, the culprit wasn't soup, but bread—or, more exactly, a loaf which had advertised itself as a diet bread because it had fewer calories per slice. This was, to be sure, a factual statement, since Profile Bread was sliced a bit thinner than the competing brands from which it differed in no other significant way. The FTC, however, took umbrage at the propriety of a loaf with seven fewer calories per slice disporting itself as a boon to the weight-conscious, and ordered Continental Baking (a subsidiary of ITT) to spend 25% of one year's advertising budget on corrective announcements. The *mea culpa* period began in Sep-

1971, with Julia Meade addressing the millions involved on television:

> "Like all mothers, I'm concerned about nutritious and balanced meals. So I'd like to clear up any misunderstanding you may have about Profile bread from its advertising or even from its name . . . eating Profile will not cause you to lose weight. A reduction of seven calories is insignificant . . . "[31]

This retroactive disclaimer, unfortunately, neither kept two irate California dieters from filing a $100 million class action law suit, nor the FTC from taking on another Continental-ITT loaf—in this case, Wonder.[32] And here the FTC found itself fully immersed in the complexities of psychologically-based manipulation, confronting such slogans as "Helps Build Strong Bodies Twelve Ways," "These Are Your Wonder Bread Years," and an evocative "How Big Do You Want to Be?" At issue here were two questions. First, did Wonder build strong bodies in precisely twelve ways? As always when experts become involved, opinions vary. In an ad entitled "An Important Message to Every Mother," Continental-ITT reassuringly stood by its twelve. For its part, the FTC called in a battery of witnesses to allege the opposite, including a certain Dr. Michael Latham of Cornell, who posited a causal link between childhood Wonder consumption and middle-aged heart disease—clearly not one of Wonder's twelve ways.[33]

But of far greater import than the twelve-ways disputation was the FTC's attack upon the alleged psychological effects of Wonder's advertising. To simplify, the Commission argued (correctly) that the real power of advertising lies not just in its claims—true, false, meaningless, or irrelevant—but also in its ability to affect consumer preferences by surrounding products with a diffuse, slowly-cumulating aura of superiority. In technical parlance, this is known as the "halo effect," and for corrective advertising to work, it had to tarnish halos. So the FTC contended that the Wonder themes, by virtue of repetition, if not of content, left the impression of superiority, even though no such claim had been made. Further, at least according to one invited expert witness, such advertising influenced a great deal more than the bread market. Recounted *Advertising Age:*

> Dr. Albert J. Solnit referred mainly to a Wonder bread "growth sequence" commercial showing a child sprouting from a 6-year-old size to a 12-year-old size in 30 seconds.
>
> "The child from 6 to 12 takes this as a promise . . .
>
> "When the child finds there's no truth in such dramatic growth, he begins to feel that the adult world is deceitful . . . "[34]

Alternatively, according to Dr. Solnit, a Yale psychologist, "I expect that some will have another fear, that the growth will become so exuberant that they will grow out of control and become giants. Or that they will not grow at all if they don't get the product."[35]

Either way, it seemed no American child might escape without permanent emotional scarring or grievously impaired moral sensibilities.

In the end, an FTC administrative law judge refused to sanction the penalty. Other corporations and agencies, though, didn't fare quite so well. A few examples will suffice, specimens chosen to demonstrate how prosecution of product claims drove advertisers into the therapeutic. The FTC ordered corrective advertising for Geritol. J. B. Williams complied, but also started a new campaign with variations on the "I'm in love with you/me/us/life theme, so I take Geritol" and, later, "My wife, I think I'll keep her." Analgesics: a required statement that they're all alike, followed by a new emphasis on "old-folks" advertising by several brands. Listerine: product and curative claims dropped in favor of "More than a Mouthwash." The list goes on, an inventory of judgments and claims and extended prosecutions which once prompted an exasperated commissioner to ask: "When does the truth become unfair?"[36]

Sometime in the 1970s, it would seem. And, early in the

decade, *Advertising Age* offered a few examples of ads which the FTC might find acceptable:[37]

For banks:

> THE MONEY YOU BORROW FROM FIRST NATIONAL BANK IS MADE BY THE UNITED STATES GOVERNMENT, FOR THE MOST PART.
> We suppose that an occasional bad twenty slips by us, but we try real hard to pass out only the genuine article, made and backed (but not guaranteed to retain its value) by the U.S. Government.
> First National Bank, Member FDIC, like most other banks.

For travel:

> COME TO DALLAS!
> After all, everybody's got to be somewhere, and you might as well be here.

For gasoline:

> It will run most cars—if they will run on gasoline in the first place, and if they will run at all in the second place, and if they have all the other necessary parts and equipment in the third place.
> If *you* have a car that runs on gasoline and meets all those other qualifications, we can't see any real point in your not trying our product.

And, last but certainly not least, for Wonder Bread:

> WE'LL GIVE YOU A SLICE OF OUR BREAD IF YOU GIVE US A SLICE OF YOURS.
> We bake Wonder bread, and we're proud of our product. No other baker can make that claim.
> Not that Wonder bread is better for you than most other brands, but that we're prouder of it than we are of most other brands.

In the end, the anti-advertising animus faded away. By 1974, the prime movers had all departed the agency, and the

Ford administration evinced no great ardor for continued prosecutions. Commission investigations and general hearings had turned up no revelations not available in any advertising or marketing textbook, and the evidence was beginning to cumulate that corrective advertising, even when conducted for years, had no discernible effects.[38] Ultimately, Congress reined in the Commission, which was saved in 1980 from real emasculation only by the intervention of the Carter White House. Today, corrective advertising remains an available regulatory tool, but one infrequently applied.

But the great consumerist crusade of the 1970s did leave one enduring legacy concerning advertising: a clear demonstration that, as discourse, it cannot be controlled—perhaps not even understood—by the traditional tools of rational analysis. Its effects can be neither measured nor controlled with any real confidence. But, perhaps, its larger meanings can be understood.

MEANINGS

But it may be asked what we have adopted in place of those institutions, those ideas, and those customs of our forefathers which we have abandoned.

Alexis de Tocqueville
Democracy in America

Therapy: Any form of service rendered to suffering human beings.

A Consumer's Guide to Psychotherapy

To the extent that we live in a civilization at once image-obsessed, media-dominated, and psychologically-defined, the advertisement stands as a metaphor, indeed as a distillate, of our common life. To the extent that we accept, adopt, or acquiesce to its meanings and accept its ministrations, the advertisement defines us. Neil Postman has written that: "The television commercial is not at all about the character of the products to be consumed. It is about the character of the consumers of products."[1] What is true of television advertising is no less appropriately applied to the other media. More and more, the ethos of the advertisement—its values and its offerings both material and psychological—penetrates every aspect of our private and public lives. And, more and more, the advertisement redefines discourse.

But advertising is, of course, no isolated phenomenon. It forms, instead, but one part of an interlocking system of such manipulations: entertainment, politics, education, even religion. That politicians and preachers advertise matters very little; that the content of their programs and their theologies comes increasingly to resemble that appropriate to advertising matters a great deal. Thought, policy, morality, even reality itself, increasingly comes to be redefined as that which can be packaged by the media, with the advertisement by far the most attractive, the most concentrated, and the most ever-present package.

Of course, "reality" doesn't go away simply because we confuse it with imagery or wish it gone with therapeutics. "Reality" remains: the hydrogen bombs, the trillion-dollar deficits, the terrorist crazies, the starving and probably useless mass millions, the coming ecological disasters. No doubt it will all some day catch up with a civilization trying to live, as the theologian Reinhold Niebuhr once phrased it, "as a paradise of domestic security suspended in a global hell."[2] What matters, for the moment, however, is why we have chosen to deal with realities both public and private, national and global, by means of therapeutic image manipulation—why we have permitted, indeed encouraged, the creation of an intricate, mutually sustaining set of manipulative systems, in which the advertisement must be judged the exemplar.

A quarter century ago, historian Daniel Boorstin accurately described what American civilization was turning into. In his introduction to *The Image*, he wrote:

> In this book I describe the world of our making; how we have used our wealth, our literacy, our technology and our progress, to create the thicket of unreality which stands between us and the facts of life. . . .
> The making of the illusions which flood our experience has become the business of America. . . . I am thinking not only of advertising and public relations and political rhetoric, but all the activities which purport to inform and comfort and improve and educate and elevate us . . . [3]

For Boorstin, America was becoming a nation not only image and illusion-obsessed, but also worshipful of the processes by which those phenomena were contrived. He viewed this process as a fundamental shift away from ideals and toward images: away from the permanent and binding, toward the manipulable and convenient. He saw in advertising, not simply the glorification of "materialistic" values, but a form of existential dishonesty:

> The momentous sign of the rise of image-making, and its displacement of ideals is, of course, the rise of advertising. Nothing has been more widely misunderstood. Daring not to admit that we may be our own deceivers, we anxiously seek some one to accuse of deceiving us. . . . We refuse to believe that advertising men are at most our collaborators, helping us to make illusions for ourselves. . . . We think it has meant an increase in untruthfulness. In fact, it has meant a reshaping of our very concept of truth.[4]

This reshaping Boorstin defines with chilling succinctness as a shift from any form of objectivity to emphasis on credibility, believability: "All of us . . . are daily less interested in whether something is a fact than in whether it is convenient that it should be believed."[5] This standard of "convenience" has come to dominate our lives, he suggests, not because we are stupid or evil, but because we can afford it.

True, we can, or could. In either case, Boorstin's explanation for the rise of this phenomenon seems a bit simplistic. To be able to afford something is not always the same as to want it. In order to understand why this inter-locking latticework of illusion and imagery became not only possible but essential, it is necessary to posit something which may seem, at first encounter, preposterous:

We are living in a tyranny.

For decades now, perhaps near a century, we have been living in one of the most pernicious tyrannies of all time: the tyranny of the psychological. By this I mean something at once obvious and exceedingly complex. Our dominant standards of judgement and value are psychological. We evaluate, we accept or reject, we admit or deny, on the basis of how we feel. Further, we accept that our feelings, our emotional responses to the world and all its realities ought to be the proper, indeed the sole, legitimate response. Whatever the influence of religion, how many of us really worry about what God or the priest or the rabbi is thinking? For the most part, we regard religion as an occasional source of comfort and solace, i.e., as therapeutic. And, no matter how seriously we consume our religion, how many of us would really desire to live in a theologically-defined society, let alone a theocracy? Whatever the influence of political thought, how many of us really worry about adhering to the principles of Thomas Jefferson or Karl Marx or John Kennedy or even Ronald Reagan or Mario Cuomo? Political life has become, for the vast majority, an activity indistinguishable from entertainment, and for a vocal few, a therapeutic means of "feeling good about yourself" by "getting involved." Today, even the word "ideology" (whose literal meaning is "the study of ideas") is discredited, and how many of us would desire to live in an ideologically-defined society?

We have, in short, substituted psychological criteria for those of religion, politics and ideas, to say nothing of the pseudo-criteria of race, class, and caste. We have substituted an inner tyranny for the older, external tyrannies of tribe and state and priesthood. We have, to borrow a phrase from Erich Fromm, escaped from freedom. Fromm, a neo-Freudian humanistic psychiatrist, well understood the terrible psychic burdens of freedom and correctly saw in the political fanaticisms of our century an extremely seductive evasion. But he, and we, have sensed far less clearly that the psychological, the psychotherapeutic, could itself become tyrannical, an endless totalitarianism of self which blurs the boundaries between private and public, real and imaginary, true and credible. And it is a totalitarianism self-sustained and abetted by a psychological/psychotherapeutic establishment whose ideas and personnel have come to suffuse this civilization's life.

Perhaps this twentieth-century escape from freedom into the psychologically-defined self and the attendant cultural and political dominance of psychological practitioners was inevitable. By the 1920s, urban life had grown exceedingly complex, the older verities shattered by war, by progress, by science, by newness. The confluence of liberation from older limits and the destruction of older principles produced an historically unprecedented situation, which called forth an historically unprecedented arrangement of human personality. As Kenneth Keniston has written:

> Our society offers no "package deals" in which one choice takes care of most of the rest. . . .
>
> Replacing the more total identifications of the past are ever more partial, selective, and incomplete identifications. . . .
>
> [T]he only workable solution for most Americans is to attempt a unique integration of their own lives, an idiosyncratic synthesis . . . [6]

Keniston called this project the "privatization of Utopia"—the attempt to create a satisfactory existence by shopping among the partial alternatives, and mixing and matching according to taste or whim. Ernest Dichter described it as the process by which countless millions attempt to furnish their little capsules of isolation, with the advertiser, as just one more professional changer of human nature, helping those millions to "resolve the misery of choice."

But even Utopia (a word which literally means "nowhere") can't be privatized, certainly not along psychological standards. The result of this project has been, not Utopia, but a new personality style described by Robert Jay Lifton as protean:

> The protean style of self-process, then, is characterized by an interminable series of experiments and explorations—some shallow, some profound—each of which may be readily abandoned in favor of still new psychological quests. . . . It extends to all areas of human experience—to political as well as sexual behavior, to the holding and promulgating of ideas and to the general organization of lives.[7]

For Lifton, this style seemed less pathological than adaptive, a proper response to life in a civilization offering both countless possibilities and omnipresent dangers.

And, given this style of personality, this organization based only on non-commitment, transience, and whim, what would be more logical than the construction of a cultural apparatus which both serves and reinforces? What could be more fitting for such "protean" human beings than a culture in which nothing save their inner (and always transient) estates need be deemed true, or even important?

What could be more logical . . . and more suicidal?

As Christopher Lasch has well written, "Now that the public world has receded into the shadows, we can see more clearly than before the extent of our need of it."[8] Shared values, common purposes, and ultimately, as Lasch puts it, "belief in a world that survives its inhabitants," all matter greatly.[9] But the tyranny of the psychological destroys the public, the common world, just as surely as, in the end, it destroys the integrity of its devotees. It destroys not only by denying the objective existence and inherent worth of the public world, but also by subjecting it to its own imperious categories.

This is to say: just as we have, as a species, learned that certain notions—civilization and racism, fascism, totalitarianism—cannot co-exist, it is time to learn that civilization and the tyranny of the psychological cannot co-exist. Over the past few years, this realization has begun to draw on increasing numbers of people.

The realization has three parts. First is the simple fact that the disciplines of psychology and psychiatry have lost their pretensions to scientific status. A science, any science, requires an agreed-upon, verifiable body of fundamental fact. Yet beyond certain matters of brain physiology, psychology agrees on nothing. It offers, instead, a chaos of competing and conflicting systems: Freudian, neo-Freudian, post-Freudian, anti-Freudian, eclectic, humanistic, behavioral, and on and on. There is, in short, precious little truth to be had, only a numbing collection of paradigms and techniques.

Second, the very vocabularies of psychologically- and psychotherapeutically-based discourse have broken down. Writing in the *Yale Review*, psychiatrist Fred Bloom suggested that "it is possible for psychoanalysis to develop in regressive or degenerate forms."[10] He criticized the mechanistic over-simplification, the evasiveness, the compression, and the unreality of much contemporary psychotherapy:

> Brevity is the one thing all the new therapies have in common. They arrive fully formed, easily managed, and ready for use. . . . The patient learns a dazzlingly simplified rationale, an order and a complete language to impose upon his own experience and to interpose between himself and the larger world.[11]

In other words, not only have ads become therapies, but therapies have taken on the characteristics of ads. A degenerating set of disciplines and pseudo-disciplines can now do little more than provide its consumers with catchy slogans and all-purpose invocations: everything from "inferiority complex" (a venerable category) to the newer mantras of "authenticity" and "self-fulfillment" and whatever else appears on the market from time to time.

But more than psychiatrists have noticed the deadness of psychological vocabularies. In recent works such as *Habits of the Heart* and *New Rules,* both authors and interviewees stress the limitations of the vocabularies available to express their goals and ideals. These sociological studies, as well as daily life, increasingly reveal a civilization which has, just as it did a century ago, outgrown its categories of thought.

If the psychological discipline has fragmented beyond all coherence, and if the vocabularies available to human beings no longer suffice to express their realities, perhaps the beginnings of the liberation from the psychological is underway. There seems to be a rising interest in (one hesitates to say increase in) what is currently known as "commitment," the making of permanent obligations to that which exists independently of oneself. "Protean Man," for whom all permanence is anathema, cannot cherish such things; the "American Narcissus," unable to distinguish between himself and the world, cannot conceive of them. But, increasingly, we are coming to recognize, as Daniel Yankelovich once put it:

> The error of replacing self-denial with a duty-to-self ethic has proven nearly fatal, for nothing has subverted self-fulfill-

ment more thoroughly than self-indulgence. . . . The pervasive influence of self-psychology in its various forms has led to a conception of the human self that underlies the most misleading premises of the search for self-fulfillment . . . the assumption of the self as private consciousness, the more private the more real.[12]

And nowhere is this new consciousness of the human importance of ties to that which exists outside of one self more apparent than in the ads.

Take a look. In 1986, they're peddling family, community, nation, pride in giving, pride in belonging, integrity.

But for how long?

EPILOGUE

There are passions for the ties to duty and honor that are
as basic to human nature as sexuality.

Fred A. Bloom
Psychiatric Help 5¢

This descent into a vast triviality . . .

Neil Postman
Amusing Ourselves to Death

In 1984, a book entitled *The Image Makers: Power and Persuasion
on Madison Avenue* appeared. As a study of advertising, the book
accomplished little. But as a piece of evidence, the book has a
vital significance. Rarely, if ever, has Daniel Boorstin's dictum
that advertising is, at best, our collaborator in fabricating
images and lies been so clearly displayed.

The author of *The Image Makers,* William Meyers, may have
intended his book as the 1980s' *Hidden Persuaders.* Certainly,
his book rivalled Packard's in its superficiality of research and
paucity of analytic thought. In his introduction, Meyers
offered a paean to Packard:

> In the late 1950s, sociologist Vance Packard shocked the
> nation with a searing exposé of the advertising industry called
> *The Hidden Persuaders.* . . . The author's indictment revealed
> many of Ad Alley's darkest secrets. . . . Packard concluded his
> controversial study with a cautionary note. If the advertising
> business was left unchecked, he warned, it would eventually
> run our lives.
>
> Today, almost three decades after *The Hidden Persuaders* was
> first published, Vance Packard's stinging prophesy has, for the
> most part, come true.[1]

According to Meyers, advertising, due largely to ever-more sophisticated psychographic manipulations, now exerts a control undreamed of in Packard's day. As evidence of this new power, Meyers cites VALS. He seems to regard its categories as nearly infallible, and Madison Avenue as correspondingly omnipotent.

And yet, according to Meyers (a former journalist who once covered advertising), Madison Avenue is also losing its grip by "failing to communicate effectively" with what he describes as "a difficult and demanding group"—the Baby Boom generation.[2] He blames this failure upon a superficial profession's inability to grasp the enormity and permanence of the changes which this group has wrought upon civilization. Borrowing freely from pop sociology and psychology, as well (apparently) as from his own experiences, he describes this wonderful culture:

> After experiencing an adolescence filled with protest, drugs, free love, and rock music, they have brought an entirely new set of values and attitudes to mainstream American society . . . the five I's: innovation, introspection, individuality, intellect, and integrity. They care as much about preserving the wilderness and world peace as they do about achieving material comfort or success.[3]

Meyers refers to these people as the counter-cultural class, the Vietnam generation, and the "Superclass" (a borrowing from Landon Y. Jones's *Great Expectations*). But mostly, he borrows from VALS, calling the Baby Boomers-turned-adult the "Societally Conscious Achievers." (Interestingly, the VALS typology has no such category; Meyers has created a hybrid of "Societally Conscious" and "Achievers.") If by this he means men and women who have learned to balance the demands of inner and outer life, then the proper VALS terminology is "Integrated," a group which, according to VALS, comprises about 2 percent of the adult population and fails to constitute an exploitable market segment. In Meyer's schema, however, there exists millions upon millions of these new heroes, a mass which, Meyers seems to feel, constitutes the last best hope of man.

After a brief survey of a few snippets of advertising history, Meyers moves on to a set of case studies, mostly of marketing failures. Rejecting the notion that other typologies matter much anymore, he offers continual (and, one might add, unsolicited) marketing advice on how best to capture this "Superclass." A few examples:

> The future winners in the soda business will almost certainly be those—like Seven-Up—that can communicate with the emerging Societally-Conscious majority.[4]

In praise of a certain automobile promoter:

> Unlike so many on Madison Avenue, he understood that you can't rush Societally-Conscious Achievers into a purchase. These prickly individualists need plenty of attention and information before they plunk down a penny.[5]

For fast food outlets:

> Societally-Conscious Achievers would rather munch on nachos or lo mein than on Big Macs or Whoppers. Even with Madison Avenue's magic manipulation at work, it's questionable whether members of the emerging superclass can be persuaded to get into their cars and drive down the interstate for a hamburger and fries. If they want to flourish . . . McDonald's and Burger King are going to have to change their way of thinking about food and the people they serve it to.[6]

On women:

> Despite obvious signs of psychographic change, Madison Avenue and its packaged goods clients have done surprisingly little to improve their reputations among inner-directed females. . . .[7]

The examples could fill a few more pages, but the pattern is clear, and evocative. Mr. Meyers, clearly a member of the most heavily psychologized generation in human history, has been raised from birth on an intellectual and spiritual diet composed of self-righteousness and manipulation, *simultaneously deploring advertising's great power and suggesting—indeed demanding—new therapeutic ministrations, new panderings to the megalomania and narcissism of a probably imaginary "Superclass."*

And yet . . . If there is to be a break with the tyranny of the psychological, who is to do it? In this century, at least, that must be the task of the Baby Boom generation, surely among the least qualified group imaginable for such an undertaking. Can the first generation in human history raised from birth on a steady force-feeding of therapeutic manipulation seriously be expected to, at generational midpassage, change its ways so drastically? Or does the future correspond more closely to Meyers' prediction that "undoubtedly, Ad Alley . . . will soon come up with a scheme that persuades skeptical baby boomers to purchase enthusiastically and without cynicism."[8] After all, asserts Mr. Meyers, "The psycho-salesmen always seem to get their way."[9]

Perhaps. But then, it might with profit be asked:

As the millennium wanes, who are the "psycho-salesmen"?

And who exactly is selling what to whom?

NOTES

INTRODUCTION

[1]Otto Kleppner with Stephen A. Greyser, *Advertising Procedure,* 6th ed. (Englewood Cliffs: Prentice-Hall, 1977), 3.

[2]For two classic general studies of the dynamics of mass communications, see Carl Hovland, Irving Janis, and Harold Kelly, *Communication and Persuasion: Psychological Studies of Opinion Change* (New Haven: Yale University Press, 1953) and Leon Festinger, *A Theory of Cognitive Dissonance* (Stanford: Stanford University Press, 1953). For more general studies, see Robert N. Bostrum, *Persuasion* (Englewood Cliffs: Prentice-Hall, 1983) and Robert B. Cialdini, *Influence* (New York: Morrow, 1984). For a more advertising-oriented approach, see George N. Gordon, *Persuasion: The Theory and Practice of Manipulative Communication,* Studies in Public Communication, A. William Bluem, General Editor (New York: Hastings House, 1971).

[3]Michael Schudson, *Advertising, the Uneasy Persuasion: Its Dubious Impact on American Life* (New York: Basic, 1984), 3. See also Herbert E. Krugman, "The Impact of Television Advertising: Learning without Involvement," *Public Opinion Quarterly* 27 (1965), 349–356.

[4]Raymond A. Bauer, "The Obstinate Audience: The Influence Process from the Point of View of Social Communication," *American Psychologist* 19 (May 1964), 319–328.

[5]Leo Bogart, *The Age of Television: A Study of the Viewing Habits and the Impact of Television in America,* 2nd ed. (New York: Ungar, 1958), 209.

[6]See Robert Griffith, "The Selling of America: The Advertising Council and American Politics 1942–1960," *Business History Review* 57 (Autumn 1983), 388–412.

[7]Quoted in David Ogilvy, *Confessions of an Advertising Man* (New York: Atheneum, 1963), 159–160. The story appears in numerous other sources with minor variations.

THE AMERICAN AD

[1]Samuel Johnson, "The Art of Advertising," quoted in James P. Wood, *The Story of Advertising* (New York: Ronald Press, 1958), 74.

²David M. Potter, *People of Plenty: Economic Abundance and the American Character* (Chicago: University of Chicago Press, 1954), 166–168.

³See Daniel Boorstin, *The Americans: The Democratic Experience* (New York: Random House, 1973), 107–129.

⁴Quoted in Stephen Fox, *The Mirror Makers: A History of American Advertising and Its Creators* (New York: Morrow, 1984), 26.

⁵For the best recent history see Fox, *The Mirror Makers*. For older accounts of varying degrees of reliability, see Wood, *The Story of Advertising;* Frank Presbrey, *The History and Development of Advertising* (Garden City: Doubleday, 1929); Frank B. Rowsome, *They Laughed When I Sat Down to Play* (New York: Bonanza Books, 1959); and E. S. Turner, *The Shocking History of Advertising!* (New York: Dutton, 1953). For an interesting account of early advertising, see Chalmers Lowell Pancoast, *Trail Blazers of Advertising,* "Getting and Spending: The Consumer's Dilemma" Series, Leon Stein, Advisory Editor (New York: Arno Reprint, 1976). For a recent business history, see Daniel Pope, *The Making of Modern Advertising* (New York: Basic, 1983).

⁶Quoted in Wood, *Story of Advertising,* 136.

⁷See Ralph M. Hower, *The History of an Advertising Agency: N. W. Ayer and Son at Work 1869–1939* (Cambridge: Harvard University Press, 1939).

⁸Otis Pease, *The Responsibilities of American Advertising: Private Control and Public Influence 1920–1940,* Yale Publications in American Studies #2, David Horne, ed. (New Haven: Yale University Press, 1958), 7.

⁹John Gunther, *Taken at the Flood: The Story of Albert D. Lasker* (New York: Harper & Bros., 1960), 56.

¹⁰John O'Toole, *The Trouble with Advertising* (New York: Times Books, 1980), 10.

¹¹Gunther, *Taken at the Flood,* 58.

¹²O'Toole, *The Trouble with Advertising,* 11.

¹³*Ibid.,* 78.

¹⁴Quoted in Fox, *The Mirror Makers,* 54.

¹⁵Claude C. Hopkins, *My Life in Advertising* (Advertising Publications Reprint of 1927 Edition, 1966), 183–184.

¹⁶James R. Mock and Cedric Wilson, *Words that Won the War: The Story of the Committee on Public Information* (New York: Russell & Russell, 1939), 4.

¹⁷George Creel, *How We Advertised America* (New York: Arno Press Reprint of 1920 Harper & Bros. Edition, 1972), 156. See also U.S.

Committee on Public Information, *The Creel Report: Complete Report of the Chairman of the Committee on Public Information 1917-1918-1919* (New York: Da Capo Press Reprint of 1919 U.S. Government Edition, 1972). See also David M. Kennedy, *Over Here: The First World War and American Society* (New York: Oxford University Press, 1980), 45–92.

¹⁸Quoted in Rowsome, *They Laughed,* 165.

¹⁹Gerard Lambert, *All Out of Step: A Personal Memoir* (Garden City: Doubleday, 1956), 97.

²⁰*Ibid.* See also Gerard Lambert, "How I Sold Listerine," *Fortune,* September 1956, 168–172.

²¹Roland Marchand, *Advertising the American Dream: Making Way for Modernity 1920-1940* (Berkeley: University of California Press, 1985), 18–22.

²²Quoted in Joseph J. Seldin, *The Golden Fleece: Advertising in American Life* (New York: Macmillan, 1963), 26.

²³Quoted in Fox, *The Mirror Makers,* 117.

²⁴Pease, *Responsibilities of American Advertising,* 20.

²⁵Bruce Barton, *The Man Nobody Knows: A Discovery of the Real Jesus* (Indianapolis: Bobbs-Merrill, 1924), 13.

²⁶*Ibid.,* 143, 146. For a more sympathetic treatment, see T. J. Jackson Lears, "From Salvation to Self-Realization: Advertising and the Therapeutic Roots of the Consumer Culture," in Richard Wightman Fox and T. J. Jackson Lears, eds., *The Culture of Consumption: Critical Essays in American History 1880-1980* (New York: Pantheon, 1983), 27–38. See also Leo P. Ribuffo, "Jesus Christ as Business Statesman: Bruce Barton and The Selling of Corporate Capitalism," *American Quarterly* 33 (Summer 1981), 206–231.

²⁷Marchand, *Advertising the American Dream,* 323–324. See also Ray Sheldon and Egmont Arens, *Consumer Engineering: A New Technique for Prosperity,* "Getting and Spending: The Consumer's Dilemma" Series, Leon Stein, Advisory Editor (New York: Arno Press Reprint of 1932 Edition, 1936). For a contemporary treatment by a radical-left former advertising man see James Rorty, *Our Master's Voice: Advertising,* "Getting and Spending: The Consumer's Dilemma" Series, Leon Stein, Advisory Editor, (New York: Arno Press Reprint of 1934 Edition, 1976).

²⁸Geoffrey Perrett, *Days of Sadness, Years of Triumph, The American People 1939-1945* (Madison: University of Wisconsin Press, 1985), 390. See also Frank W. Fox, *Madison Avenue Goes to War: The Strange Military Career of American Advertising 1941-1945* (Provo: Brigham Young University Press, 1975) and Raymond Rubicam, "Advertis-

ing," in Jack Goodman, ed., *While You Were Gone: A Report on Wartime Life in the United States* (New York: Simon & Schuster, 1946), 421–426.

[29]Quoted in John Morton Blum, *V Was for Victory: Politics and American Culture during World War II* (New York: Harcourt Brace Jovanovich, 1976), 65. See also Richard Lingeman, *Don't You Know There's a War On? The American Home Front 1941–1945* (New York: Putnam, 1970), 291–297.

[30]Wood, *The Story of Advertising*, 444.

[31]"Advertising Licks Its Chops," *Business Week*, Feb. 16, 1952, 152.

HUCKSTERS AND PSYCHOLOGISTS

[1]Morton White, *Social Thought in America: The Revolt against Formalism* (Boston: Beacon Press, 1947); Henry F. May, *The End of American Innocence* (New York: Knopf, 1959). See also T. J. Jackson Lears, *No Place of Grace: Antimodernism and the Transformation of American Culture 1880–1920* (New York: Pantheon, 1981) and John Higham, "The Reorientation of American Culture: the 1890s," in John Higham, *Writing American History: Essays in Modern Scholarship* (Bloomington: Indiana University Press, 1970), 73–103.

[2]Thomas J. Haskell, *The Emergence of Professional Social Science: The American Social Science Association and the Nineteenth Century Crisis of Authority* (Urbana: University of Illinois Press, 1977), 1. See also James Deese, *American Freedom and the Social Sciences*, Critical Assessments of Contemporary Psychology Series, Daniel N. Robinson, ed. (New York: Columbia University Press, 1985).

[3]David S. Noble, *America by Design: Science, Technology, and the Rise of Corporate Capitalism*, Foreword by Christopher Lasch (New York: Knopf, 1977), xxvi. See also Samuel Haber, *Efficiency and Uplift: Scientific Management in the Progressive Era* (Chicago: University of Chicago Press, 1964) and Loren Baritz, *The Servants of Power: A History of the Use of Social Science in American Industry* (Middletown: Wesleyan Unviersity Press, 1960).

[4]Otis Pease, *The Responsibilities of American Advertising: Private Control and Public Influence 1920–1940*, Yale Publications in American Studies #2, David Horne, ed. (New Haven: Yale University Press, 1958), 34.

[5]"Ads You'll Never See," *Business Week*, September 21, 1957, 31.

[6]Albert T. Poffenberger, *Psychology in Advertising* (London: Albert T. Shaw, 1928), passim.

[7]Walter Dill Scott, *The Psychology of Advertising* (Boston: Small, Maynard, 1908), Frontispiece. See also Walter Dill Scott, *The Theory and Practice of Advertising* (Boston: Small, Maynard, 1903).

[8]Scott, *Psychology of Advertising*, 2, 404.

[9]Michael McMahon, "An American Courtship: Psychologists and Advertising Theory in the Progressive Era," *American Studies* 13 (Fall 1972), 8. For a variant treatment see Merle Curti, "The Changing Concept of 'Human Nature' in the Literature of American Advertising," *Business History Review* 41 (Winter 1967), 335–367.

THE COMMODITY SELF

[1]Stephen Fox, *The Mirror Makers: A History of American Advertising and Its Creators* (New York: Morrow, 1984), 85.

[2]Roland Marchand, *Advertising the American Dream: Making Way for Modernity 1920–1940* (Berkeley: University of California Press, 1985), 13.

[3]Christopher Lasch, *The Culture of Narcissism: American Life in an Age of Diminishing Expectations* (New York: Norton, 1979), 73.

[4]See Michael Schudson, *Advertising, the Uneasy Persuasion: Its Dubious Impact on American Society* (New York: Basic, 1984), 209–233.

[5]*Ibid.*, 175–176.

[6]Stuart Ewen, *Captains of Consciousness: Advertising and the Social Roots of the Consumer Culture* (New York: McGraw-Hill, 1976), 45. See also Stuart and Elizabeth Ewen, *Channels of Desire: Mass Media and the Shaping of the American Consciousness* (New York: McGraw-Hill, 1982).

[7]Ewen, *Captains of Consciousness*, 37.

[8]See Marchand, *Advertising the American Dream*, 206–284.

[9]Ewen, *Captains of Consciousness*, 69.

[10]*Ibid.*, 33

[11]*Ibid.*, 131–132.

THE FIFTIES ... AND A CAVEAT

[1]Joseph J. Seldin, *The Golden Fleece* (New York: Macmillan, 1963), 193–194.

[2]David Ogilvy, *Confessions of an Advertising Man* (New York: Atheneum, 1963), 84; Jerry Della Femina with Charles Sopkin, *From Those Wonderful Folks Who Gave You Pearl Harbor: Front-Line Dispatches from the Advertising Wars* (New York: Simon & Schuster, 1970), 28.

[3]Sigmund Freud, *Civilization and Its Discontents*, translated and edited by James Strachey (New York: Norton, 1961), 17.

FASTER THAN THE EYE CAN SEE

[1]Gay Talese, "Most Hidden Hidden Persuaders," *New York Times Magazine*, January 12, 1958, 59.

[2]"Subliminal Ad is Transmitted in Test but Scores No Popcorn Sales," *Advertising Age*, January 20, 1958, 1.

[3]Ibid.; "Subliminal Ad Shows in Capital," *New York Times*, January 14, 1958, 66.

[4] " 'Hidden Sell' Technique Is Almost Here," *Life Magazine*, March 31, 1958, 102–104.

[5]"ARF Checks Data on Subliminal Ads; Verdict Is 'Insufficient,'" *Advertising Age*, September 15, 1958, 50.

[6]"Subliminal TV Cited as Danger to Youth," *New York Times*, January 29, 1958, 24.

[7]Fred Danzig, "Subliminal Advertising—Today It's Just Historic Flashback for Researcher Vicary," *Advertising Age*, September 17, 1962, 72.

[8]"Diddling the Subconscious," *The Nation*, October 5, 1957, 207.

THE HIDDEN PERSUADERS

[1]Ernest van den Haag, "Madison Avenue Witchcraft," *The Commonweal*, November 29, 1957, 271.

[2]Vance Packard, "Resurvey of 'Hidden Persuaders,'" *New York Times Magazine*, May 11, 1958, 19.

[3]Elmo Roper, "How Powerful Are the Persuaders?" *Saturday Review*, October 5, 1957, 19.

[4]See Herbert Krugman, "An Historical Note on Motivation Research," *Public Opinion Quarterly* 20 (Winter 1956–1957), 719–723 and Alfred Politz, "Motivation Research from a Research Viewpoint," *Public Opinion Quarterly* 20 (Winter 1956–1957), 668–673. For more popular treatments see Lydia Strong, "They're Selling Your Unconscious," *Saturday Review*, November 13, 1954, 11–12, 60–63 and Perrin Stryker, "Motivation Research," *Fortune*, June 1956, 144–147, 222–232.

[5]Vance Packard, *The Hidden Persuaders* (New York: David McKay, 1957; Pocket Books, 1958), 1. See also Vance Packard, "The Growing Power of Admen," *Atlantic Monthly*, December 1957, 55–59 and

Vance Packard, "The Mass Manipulation of Human Behavior," *America,* December 14, 1957, 342–344.

[6]Packard, *Hidden Persuaders,* 6.

[7]*Ibid.*

[8]*Ibid.,* 61–70, 200–207.

[9]Raymond A. Bauer, "The Limits of Persuasion," *Harvard Business Review* 36 (September–October 1958), 107.

[10]Packard, *Hidden Persuaders,* 207.

THE STRATEGY OF DESIRE

[1]Ernest Dichter, *The Strategy of Desire* (Garden City: Doubleday, 1960), 135.

[2]Philip Rieff, *Freud: The Mind of the Moralist* (Garden City: Doubleday, 1955; Anchor Edition, 1961), xx, xxii.

[3]Ernest Dichter, *Handbook of Consumer Motivations: The Psychology of the World of Objects,* McGraw-Hill Series in Marketing and Advertising (New York: McGraw-Hill, 1964), 65.

[4]Vance Packard, *The Hidden Persuaders* (New York: David McKay, 1957; Pocket Books, 1958), 24.

[5]*Ibid.,* 50–57, 119–120.

[6]*Ibid.,* 24.

[7]Ernest Dichter, "Psychology in Market Research," *Harvard Business Review* 25 (Summer 1947), 432.

[8]Ernest Dichter, "A Psychological View of Advertising Effectiveness," *Journal of Marketing* 14 (July 1949), 61, 65.

[9]*Ibid.,* 66.

[10]"You Either Offer Security or Fail," *Business Week* 32, June 1951, 68–75.

[11]"Betty Crocker is Mom's 'Fuehrer,' Says Dichter Analysis of Ad Symbols," *Advertising Age,* September 13, 1965, 10.

[12]"Use Emotional Appeal to Instill Cloth Brand Loyalty, Fabric Awareness: Dichter," *Advertising Age,* January 6, 1958, 16.

[13]Dichter, *Handbook of Consumer Motivations,* 8.

[14]*Ibid.,* 6.

[15]*Ibid.,* 30, 19.

[16]Dichter, *Strategy of Desire,* 181.

[17]*Ibid.,* 152.

[18]*Ibid.,* 167.

[19]Ernest Dichter, "Discovering the 'Inner Jones,'" *Harvard Business Review* 43 (May–June 1965), 7.

[20]*Ibid.*, 8.

[21]Dichter, *Strategy of Desire*, 264–265.

[22]*Ibid.*, 273.

[23]Ernest Dichter, *Motivating Human Behavior* (New York: McGraw-Hill, 1971), 10.

[24]Quoted in Joseph Newman, *Motivation Research and Marketing Management* (Boston: Harvard University Graduate School of Business Administration, 1957), 213.

[25]Dichter, *Handbook of Consumer Motivations*, 149.

IDENTITY

[1]Erik Erikson, *Childhood and Society*, 2nd ed. (New York: Norton, 1950), 279.

THE GREAT DEBATE

[1]Martin Mayer, *Madison Avenue U.S.A.* (New York: Harper & Bros., 1958), 54.

[2]*Ibid.*, 53.

[3]Rosser Reeves, *Reality in Advertising* (New York: Knopf, 1961), 34.

[4]*Ibid.*, 47–48.

[5]*Ibid.*, 52.

[6]*Ibid.*, 121.

[7]David Ogilvy, *Confessions of an Advertising Man* (New York: Atheneum, 1962; Ballantine Books, 1971), 87–88. See also David Ogilvy, *Blood, Brains, and Beer: The Autobiography of David Ogilvy* (New York: Atheneum, 1978) and David Ogilvy, *Ogilvy on Advertising* (New York: Crown, 1983).

[8]Ogilvy, *Confessions*, 103.

[9]The ad itself ran only once, in the April 21, 1956 issue of *The New Yorker*. For professional reaction, see *Printer's Ink*, April 27, 1956, 74 and *Advertising Age*, February 23, 1956, 1.

[10]Reeves, *Reality in Advertising*, 68.

[11]Ogilvy, *Confessions*, 84.

THE TRAINING OF THE YOUNG

[1]Landon Y. Jones, *Great Expectations: America and the Baby Boom Generation* (New York: Coward, McCann, 1980), 2.

[2]Eugene Gilbert, *Advertising and Marketing to Young People* (Pleasantville: Printer's Ink Books, 1957), 4.

[3]Joseph J. Seldin, "Selling the Kiddies," *The Nation,* October 8, 1955, 305.

[4]*Ibid.*

[5]E. S. Turner, *The Shocking History of Advertising!* (New York: Dutton, 1953), 15.

[6]"Moppets and Money," *Dun's Review,* December 1963, 55.

[7]*Ibid.*

[8]David Riesman, with Reuel Denny and Nathan Glazer, *The Lonely Crowd: A Study of the Changing American Character,* Studies in National Policy Series (New Haven: Yale University Press, 1950), 46.

[9]Martin Mayer, *Madison Avenue U.S.A.* (New York: Harper & Bros., 1958), 119–120.

CREATIVITY

[1]T. J. Jackson Lears, *No Place of Grace: Anti-Modernism in the Transformation of American Culture 1880–1920* (New York: Pantheon, 1981), xiv, xvii.

[2]"Ad World Ready for Renaissance, Brower Tells 4A's," *Advertising Age,* April 25, 1960, 70.

[3]"Ad Field Needs Renaissance Man, Declares Gribbin," *Advertising Age,* March 2, 1964, 2.

[4]Victor Navasky, "Advertising Is a Science? an Art? a Business?" *New York Times Magazine,* November 20, 1966, 168.

[5]Frank J. Prial, "Bold Approach Brings Advertising Prominence to Wells, Rich, Greene," *Wall Street Journal,* May 6, 1968, 1.

[6]Some of this work had been done at Jack Tinker, prior to the founding of WRG.

[7]Jerry Della Femina with Charles Sopkin, *From Those Wonderful Folks Who Gave You Pearl Harbor: Front-Line Dispatches from the Advertising Wars* (New York: Simon & Schuster, 1970), 101.

[8]"Bernbach, Hockaday Extol Intuition in Ads," *Advertising Age,* November 8, 1965, 54.

[9]For a more detailed, if somewhat hagiographic recounting, see Frank Rowsome, Jr., *Think Small: The Story of Those Volkswagen Ads* (Brattleboro: Stephen Green Press, 1970). See also Walter Henry Nelson, *Small Wonder: The Amazing Story of the Volkswagen* (Boston: Little, Brown, 1965).

[10]"Selling Proposition Isn't Enough," *Advertising Age*, May 29, 1961, 60.

[11]Robert Glatzer, *The New Advertising: The Great Campaigns from Avis to Volkswagen* (New York: Citadel Press, 1970), 63.

[12]"Try Harder," *Newsweek*, July 24, 1964, 77.

[13]Della Femina, *From Those Wonderful Folks*, 38.

[14]Walter Carlson, "Advertising: More Debate over 'DDB Look,'" *New York Times*, April 6, 1966, 66.

[15]Jim Gallagher, "Who Put Empathy in the Driver's Seat?" *Sponsor*, January 14, 1965, 70–71.

[16]"No. 1," *Madison Avenue*, September 1965, 26.

[17]Glatzer, *The New Advertising*, 74.

[18]*Ibid.*, 82.

[19]"Madison Avenue: See Mary Run," *Newsweek*, October 3, 1966, 82.

[20]Charles Moss, "The Wondrous World of WRG (Revisited)," *Madison Avenue*, December 1967, 15–16.

[21]Philip Siekman, "On Lovable Madison Avenue with Mary, Dick, and Stew," *Fortune*, August 1966, 142–146, 167, and Carol J. Loomis, "As the World Turns—On Madison Avenue," *Fortune*, December 1968, 114–117, 187–194.

[22]Siekman, "Lovable," 144.

[23]"Ripple Won't Do Today," *Advertising Age*, February 17, 1969, 2.

[24]"See Mary Run," 24.

[25]"What Is an Advertising Agency?" *Saturday Review*, June 17, 1970, 65.

[26]Robin C. Nelson, "Harper's Happy Hippies," *Marketing/Communications*, October 1967, 51–52.

[27]Della Femina, *From Those Wonderful Folks*, 67.

[28]Stephen Baker, "A New Type of Agency: The Advertising Boutique," *Advertising Age*, March 13, 1967, 72.

[29]Jaada Weingarten, "Mini-Sell on Madison Avenue," *Dun's Review*, July 1967, 27.

[30]"Economics, Not Creativity, Is Aim of Ad: McDonald," *Advertising Age*, March 6, 1967, 1.

[31]"Advertising's Creative Explosion," *Newsweek*, August 18, 1969, 64.

[32]Walter Carlson, "Advertising: Where to Draw the Shock Line," *New York Times*, May 8, 1966, III:16.

[33]Ernest Dichter, "Are Advertisers Losing Out on Sex Appeal?" *Advertising Age,* April 7, 1969, 70.

[34]Lee Adler, "Cashing In on the Cop-Out," *Business Horizons,* February 1970, 19–30.

[35]Don Grant, "To Handle Youth's Anti-Business Attitude, Keep Your Cool, Says 'Gap,'" *Advertising Age,* May 13, 1968, 28.

[36]"New Agencies Cited in 1967 Slump of Giants," *Wall Street Journal,* July 3, 1968, 26.

[37]Jerry Della Femina, "The Death of the Creative Revolution," *Marketing/Communications,* February 1971, 16.

[38]*Advertising Age,* January 26, 1970, 46–47.

THE MERCHANDISING OF DESPAIR

[1]*New York Times,* February 11, 1977, D-14.

[2]*Ibid.*

[3]*New York Times,* February 23, 1977, D-16.

[4]*Ibid.*

[5]*New York Times,* March 7, 1977, 53.

[6]*New York Times,* November 22, 1977, 68.

[7]*Ibid.*

[8]*New York Times,* October 13, 1977, 68.

[9]*New York Times,* December 14, 1978, D-24.

[10]Christopher Lasch, *The Culture of Narcissism: American Life in an Age of Diminishing Expectations* (New York: Norton, 1979), xv.

[11]Jerry Fields, "The Messiah Complex Revisited," *Madison Avenue,* June 1973, 32.

[12]*Ibid.* See also "The Days of Fun and Games Are Over," *Business Week,* November 10, 1973, 84.

[13]Jeremy Gury, "Requiem for the Sixties," *Madison Avenue,* January 1970, 28.

[14]"From the Age of Affluence to the Age of Alternatives," *Advertising Age,* December 3, 1973, 12.

[15]"BBDO Studies Americans' 'Me First' Sentiment," *Advertising Age,* February 26, 1979, 44; "Older Consumers Join 'Me Generation,'" *Advertising Age,* August 13, 1979, 24.

[16]"Inflation May Emerge as Ad Theme," *Advertising Age,* July 15, 1974, 16.

[17]Ralph Gray, "Detroit Rolls Out Quickly with 'Buy Now' Ad Effort," *Advertising Age,* November 11, 1974, 1, 74.

[18]Raphael Patai, *Myth and Modern Man* (Englewood Cliffs: Prentice-Hall, 1972), 244.

[19]*Ibid.*

[20]Harry W. McMahon, "Bank Advertising Has Its Troubles," *Advertising Age,* July 13, 1970, 82.

[21]"Easy on 'Grandpa Ads,'" *Advertising Age,* June 27, 1977, 14.

[22]Ellis Weiner, "Patriotic Spot (60 secs.)," *The New Yorker,* June 30, 1980, 31.

THE STATE OF THE ART

[1]Edwin Diamond and Stephen Bates, *The Spot: The Rise of Political Advertising on Television* (Cambridge: MIT Press, 1984), 9–10.

[2]See Frank Deford, *Lite Reading: The Lite Beer from Miller Commercial Scrap Book* (New York: Penguin, 1984). See also William Flanagan, "The Charge of the Lite Brigade, *Esquire,* July 18, 1978, 73–83.

[3]Sandra Salman, "Those Precocious Jeans Ads," *New York Times,* December 1, 1980, D-1.

[4]"The Bum's Rush in Advertising," *Time,* December 1, 1980, 95.

[5]"Precocious."

[6]"Time for 'Survival' Ads?" *Advertising Age,* August 20, 1979, 16.

[7]Lee Iacocca and William Novak, *Iacocca: An Autobiography* (New York: Bantam, 1984), 222–224.

[8]*Ibid.,* 273.

[9]Michael Schudson, *Advertising, the Uneasy Persuasion: Its Dubious Impact on American Life* (New York: Basic, 1984), 10.

[10]For general assessment of the problem of marketing to women see Rena Bartos, *The Moving Target: What Every Marketer Should Know about Women* (New York: Free Press, 1982) and Rosemary Scott, *The Female Consumer* (New York: John Wiley, 1976). For studies of sexual roles in advertising see Alice E. Courtney and Thomas W. Whipple, *Sex Stereotyping in Advertising* (Lexington: D. C. Heath, 1983) and Erving Goffman, *Gender Advertisements* (New York: Harper & Row, 1976).

[11]Caroline Mayer, "Advertisers Heat Up Cold War with TV Parodies of Soviets," *Washington Post,* December 22, 1985, K-1.

[12]"How Not to Recruit," *Advertising Age,* July 26, 1971, 16.

[13]"The Army: Woodstock in Combat Boots?" *Advertising Age,* April 23, 1973, 18.

[14]"Army Needs Professional Ad Corps," *Advertising Age,* April 7, 1975, 14.

[15]Richard L. Gordon, "Add $ Won't Solve Military Woes," *Advertising Age,* February 18, 1980, 1, 78.

[16]Comptroller General of the United States, *Report to the Congress: Advertising for Military Recruiting: How Effective Is It?* (Washington, D.C., U.S. Government Printing Office, 1976).

[17]Hughes Rudd, "Must Mad Ave Go to Boot Camp?" *Advertising Age,* April 25, 1977, 76.

VALS

[1]For basic marketing concepts see Philip Kotler, *Principles of Marketing,* 2nd ed. (Englewood Cliffs: Prentice-Hall, 1983).

[2]Theodore Levitt, *Innovation in Marketing: New Perspectives for Profit and Growth* (New York: McGraw-Hill, 1962), v.

[3]Theodore Levitt, *The Marketing Imagination,* expanded edition (New York: Free Press, 1986), 81–84.

[4]Al Ries and Jack Trout, *Positioning: The Battle for Your Mind* (New York: McGraw-Hill, 1981), 3.

[5]Arnold Mitchell, *The Nine American Lifestyles* (New York: Warner Books, 1983).

[6]*Ibid.,* vii, 25.

[7]*Ibid.,* 163.

THE MARKETING OF CONSCIOUSNESS

[1]Quoted in William Meyer, *The Image Makers: Power and Persuasion on Madison Avenue* (New York: Times Books, 1984), 7.

[2]See Allen Hyman and M. Bruce Johnson, *Advertising and Free Speech* (Lexington: D. C. Heath, 1976). See also E. John Kottman, "Is National Advertising Still a 'Stepchild of the First Amendment'?" *Journal of Advertising Research* 8 (Fall 1979), 6–12.

[3]Quoted in Kottman, "National Advertising," 8.

[4]*Ibid.,* 6.

[5]*Ibid.,* 11.

[6]"Let's Use Advertising Skills to Make Decency and Integrity Fashionable, Editor Urges," *Advertising Age,* February 10, 1958, 61–63.

[7]David L. Paletz, Roberta E. Pearson, and Donald L. Willis, *Politics in Public Service Advertising on Television,* Praeger Special Studies in U.S. Economic, Social, and Political Issues (New York: Praeger, 1977), 19.

[8]"Ads Get New Social Crisis Role, ANA Told," *Advertising Age,* September 16, 1968, 1.

[9]See "An Adman Battles Society's Ills," *Business Week,* September 11, 1971, 108–110 and "The Protest Workshop," *Madison Avenue,* January 1970, 10–13.

[10]"Write Your Senator . . . While You Still Have One," *Advertising Age,* June 17, 1968, 3, 3B.

[11]"Madison Avenue against the War," *Time,* July 17, 1970, 67.

[12]Thomas Whiteside, *Selling Death: Cigarette Advertising and Public Health* (New York: Liveright, 1970), 1.

[13]For coverage see Whitehead, *Selling Death.* See also A. Lee Fritschler, *Smoking and Politics: Policymaking and the Federal Bureaucracy* (Englewood Cliffs: Prentice-Hall, 1975) and Susan Wagner, *Cigarette Country* (New York: Praeger, 1972). See also S. Prakash Sethi, "Warning: Cigarette Smoking is Dangerous to Your Health," in S. Prakash Sethi, ed., *Promises of the Good Life: Social Consequences of Private Marketing Decisions,* Irwin Series in Marketing (Homewood: Irwin, 1979), 43–66.

[14]FCC Letters 67–641, Frank Kahn, ed. *Documents of American Broadcasting* (New York: Appleton-Century-Crofts, 1960), 395–397.

[15]See "The Last Cigarette Campaign," in Robert Glatzer, *The New Advertising: The Great Campaigns from Volkswagen to Avis* (New York: Citadel Press, 1970), 183–190.

[16]See Sandra J. Teel, Jesse E. Teel, and William O. Bearden, "Lessons Learned from the Broadcast Cigarette Advertising Ban," *Journal of Marketing* 43 (July 1979), 45–50. See also U.S. Federal Trade Commission, *Report to Congress Pursuant to the Public Health Cigarette Smoking Act,* December 31, 1979.

[17]U.S. Congress, House of Representatives, *Hearings before the Committee on Interstate and Foreign Commerce on Various Bills,* Series #91–12, Part 3, 91st Congress, 1st Session, 1338–1339.

CORPORATE PROTEST

[1]George A. Flanagan, *Modern Institutional Advertising* (New York: McGraw-Hill, 1967), 5.

[2]Harold H. Marquis, *The Changing Corporate Image* (American Marketing Association, 1970), 22.

[3]William D. Tyler, "Don't Pretend Your Motives Are Loftier Than They Really Are," *Advertising Age,* December 21, 1970, 27.

[4]*Ibid.*

[5]S. Prakash Sethi, *Advocacy Advertising and Large Corporations: Social Conflict, Big Business Image, the News Media, and Public Policy* (Lexington: D. C. Heath, 1975), 57. See also International Advertising Association, *Controversy Advertising: How Advertisers Present Points of View in Public Affairs* (New York: Hastings House, 1977).

[6]Rawleigh Warner and Leonard S. Silk, *Ideals in Collision: The Relationship between Business and the News Media,* The 1978 Benjamin Fairless Memorial Lectures (New York: Carnegie-Mellon University Press, 1979), 15.

[7]"Mobil Latest to Slash Gas Ads," *Advertising Age,* June 25, 1973, 1, 67.

[8]"Gasoline, Car Ads React to Shortage," *Advertising Age,* May 7, 1973, 1, 88. See also "Oil Ads Center on Corporate, TBA," *Advertising Age,* September 7, 1973, 1, 79.

[9]"Senate Asks NARB Support against 'Deceptive' Engergy Ads," *Advertising Age,* December 3, 1973, 1. See also "Oilmen Rip Bid to FTC for Proof on Energy Ads," *Advertising Age,* January 14, 1974, 1, 64 and "Energy Companies Fear New Challenges to Their 'Image' Ads," *Wall Street Journal,* March 12, 1974, 15.

[10]"Oil's Credibility Gap," *Advertising Age,* February 11, 1974, 16.

[11]Josh Levine, "Oil Companies Learn to Pick Spots," *Advertising Age,* February 4, 1980, 1.

[12]Herb Schmertz with William Novak, *Good-bye to the Low Profile: The Art of Creative Confrontation* (Boston: Little, Brown, 1986), 168.

[13]*Ibid.,* 143.

[14]*Ibid.,* 235.

ELECTING OUR KING

[1]Kathleen Hall Jamieson, *Packaging the Presidency: A History and Criticism of Presidential Campaign Advertising* (New York: Oxford University Press, 1984), 446.

[2]Larry J. Sabato, *The Rise of Political Consultants: New Ways of Winning Elections* (New York: Basic, 1980), 115. For studies of the relationship between political consultants and advertising not cited elsewhere in this chapter see Robert Bonitati, *Winning Campaigns with the New Politics,* Introduction by Rogers C. B. Morton (New York: Popular Library, 1971); Ray E. Hiebert, *et al.,* eds., *The Political Image Merchants: Strategies for the Seventies,* Foreword by Samuel J. Archibald (Washington, D.C.: Acropolis Books, 1975); Joseph Napolitan, *The*

Election Game and How to Win It (Garden City: Doubleday, 1972); James M. Perry, *The New Politics: The Expanding Technology of Political Manipulation* (New York: Clarkson Potter, 1968); and Gene Wyckoff, *The Image Candidates: American Politics in the Age of Television* (New York: Macmillan, 1968).

[3]Fred Barnes, "The Myth of Political Consultants," *The New Republic,* June 16, 1986, 19.

[4]*Ibid.,* 18.

[5]Jeff Greenfield, *Playing to Win: An Insider's Guide to Politics* (New York: Simon and Schuster, 1980), 191.

[6]Quoted in Edwin Diamond and Stephen Bates, *The Spot: The Rise of Political Advertising on Television* (Cambridge: MIT Press, 1984), 42.

[7]Terry Hynes, "Media Manipulation and Political Campaigns: Bruce Barton and the Presidential Elections of the Jazz Age," *Journalism History* 4 (Autumn 1977), 94.

[8]Sig Mickelson, *The Electric Mirror: Politics in the Age of Television* (New York: Dodd, Mead, 1972), 58.

[9]*Ibid.,* 59.

[10]Diamond and Bates, *The Spot,* 57.

[11]*Ibid.,* 58.

[12]"Advertising and Marketing," *New York Times,* November 7, 1956, 48.

[13]Diamond and Bates, *The Spot,* 129.

[14]Quoted in Robert E. Gilbert, *Television and Presidential Politics* (North Quincy: Christopher Publishing House, 1972), 215.

[15]Tony Schwartz, *The Responsive Chord* (Garden City: Doubleday Anchor, 1973), 93, 96.

[16]Garry Wills, *Nixon Agonistes: The Crisis of the Self-Made Man* (New York: Mentor, 1972), 371.

[17]Godfrey Hodgson, *America in Our Time* (Garden City: Doubleday, 1976), 365.

[18]Wills, *Nixon,* 72.

[19]Jules Witcover, *The Resurrection of Richard Nixon* (New York: Putnam's, 1970), 400.

[20]William Safire, *Before the Fall: An Insider's View of the Pre-Watergate White House* (Garden City: Doubleday, 1975), 43.

[21]John Osborne, *The Nixon Watch,* Introduction by Tom Wicker (New York: Liveright, 1970), 4–5.

[22]Joe McGinniss, *The Selling of the President 1968* (New York: Pocket Books, 1969), 193–194.

[23]*Ibid.,* 31.

[24]*Ibid.,* 126.

[25]Theordore H. White, *The Making of the President 1968* (New York: Atheneum, 1969), 134.

[26]McGinniss, *Selling of the President,* 83–84.

[27]*Ibid.,* 91–94.

[28]*Ibid.,* 116–117.

[29]Jules Witcover, *Marathon: The Pursuit of the Presidency 1972–1976* (New York: Signet, 1977), 115–116.

[30]Quoted in Kandy Stroud, *How Jimmy Won: The Victory Campaign from Plains to the White House* (New York: Morrow, 1977), 25.

[31]*Ibid.,* 26.

[32]Martin Schram, *Running for President 1976: The Carter Campaign* (New York: Stein and Day, 1977), 52.

[33]*Ibid.,* 56–57.

[34]"Huckstering the Candidates," *Newsweek,* April 12, 1976, 87.

[35]Jonathan Moore and Janet Fraser, eds., *Campaign for President: The Managers Look at '76* (Cambridge: Ballinger, 1977), 90.

[36]Phil Gailey, "Rafshoon Has Second Shot at Showing Carter," *Washington Star,* May 29, 1978, 12.

[37]*Ibid.*

[38]"Adman in the White House," *Advertising Age,* May 29, 1978, 12.

[39]Diamond and Bates, *The Spot,* 285–286.

THE FTC

[1]Robert Spero, *The Duping of the American Voter: Dishonesty and Deception in Presidential Television Advertising* (New York: Lippincott and Crowell, 1980).

[2]For a non-technical treatment of advertising law see Ivan L. Preston, *The Great American Blow-Up: Puffery in Advertising and Selling* (Madison: University of Wisconsin Press, 1975). For general histories of the FTC see Alan Stone, *Economic Regulation in the Public Interest: The Federal Trade Commission in Theory and Practice* (Ithaca: Cornell University Press, 1977) and Susan Wagner, *The Federal Trade Commission,* Praeger Library of U.S. Government Departments and Agencies, Ernest S. Griffith and Hugh Langdon Elsbree, Consulting Editors (New York: Praeger, 1971).

[3]Quoted in Wagner, *The Federal Trade Commission,* 17.

[4]Quoted in Preston, *Great American Blow-Up,* 133.

[5]George J. Alexander, *Honesty and Competition: False-Advertising Law and Policy under FTC Administration* (Syracuse: Syracuse University Press, 1967), 8.

[6]See Earl Kintner, *A Primer on the Law of Deceptive Practices* (New York: Macmillan, 1971) and Leigh R. Isaacs, "Psychological Advertising: A New Area of FTC Regulation," *Wisconsin Law Review* 4 (1972), 1097–1124. See also Ira Millstein, "The Federal Trade Commission and False Advertising," *Columbia Law Review* 64 (1964), 457–461.

[7]"Washington at Work," *Wall Street Journal,* December 8, 1961, 15.

[8]Jay Walz, "TV Commercials Face FTC Curbs," *New York Times,* March 3, 1957, 54.

[9]Bates Advertisement, *New York Times,* January 25, 1960, 54.

[10]"Court Forbids Shave in Claim of TV Ad," *New York Times,* April 6, 1965, 1, 20.

[11]See Edward F. Cox, Robert C. Fellmouth, and John E. Schurz, *"The Nader Report" on the Federal Trade Commission,* Preface by Ralph Nader (New York: Richard W. Baron, 1969).

[12]Eileen Shanahan, "Bar P nel Urges Changes in FTC or Its Abo- ı," *New York Times,* Septe₁ ₁₊r 16, 1969, 1.

Harrison Wellford, "How   ph Nader, Tricia Nixon, the ABA, and Jamie Whitten Helped 7 ı ı the FTC Around," *Washington Monthly,* October 1972, 12–13.

[14]*Ibid.,* 5.

[15]Stanley E. Cohen, "Force Advertiser to Substantiate His Ad Claims, Nader Urges FTC," *Advertising Age,* December 14, 1970, 1, 65.

[16]John D. Morris, "FTC to Order Industries to Substantiate Their Ads," *New York Times,* June 11, 1972, 1.

[17]Stanley E. Cohen, "FTC to Demand Substantiation of Ads, Supply It to Consumers," *Advertising Age,* June 14, 1971, 1, 105.

[18]Morris, "FTC to Order," 17.

[19]"Klein Sees Peril to Press in FTC's Plan on Ads," *New York Times,* June 12, 1971, 32.

[20]U.S. Congress, Senate, *Staff Report to the Federal Trade Commission on the Ad Substantiation Program,* prepared by the Honorable Frank Moss, 92nd Congress, 2nd session, iv.

[21]Richard A. Posner, *Regulation of Advertising by the FTC,* American Enterprise Institute Evaluative Studies (Washington: American Enterprise Institute, 1973), 23–24. See also Dorothy Cohen, "The FTC's Advertising Substantiation Program," *Journal of Marketing* 44 (Winter 1980), 26–35.

[22]Stanley E. Cohen, "Counter Ad Battle Continues: Nets Reject Consumer Spots," *Advertising Age,* May 1, 1972, 1, 79; "FCC Probes

for Effects of Counter Ads on Advertisers," *Advertising Age,* April 3, 1973, 1, 72; and "Free Counter Ad Proposal Will Die, Whitehead Says," *Advertising Age,* October 23, 1972, 2, 112.

[23]John Revett, "Counter Ads May Wither in Wake of High Court Ruling," *Advertising Age,* June 4, 1973, 1, 98. See also "FCC Vetoes Counter Ads for Most Product Spots," *Advertising Age,* July 1, 1974, 1, 55.

[24]See Michael T. Brandt and Ivan L. Preston, "The Federal Trade Commission's Use of Evidence to Determine Deception," *Journal of Marketing* 41 (January 1977), 54–62.

[25]"Consent Order Readied against Campbell Soup and BBDO Firms," *Wall Street Journal,* September 22, 1969, 6.

[26]Henry R. Bernstein, "FDA Still Ponders Effects of Its 'Corrective' Ads," *Advertising Age,* May 10, 1971, 16.

[27]"Geritol Ads Must Carry Disclaimer: FTC Examiner," *Advertising Age,* May 25, 1964, 1, 164.

[28]Stanley E. Cohen, "Weinberger Asserts FTC Power to Demand 'Corrective' Ads," *Advertising Age,* June 8, 1970, 112.

[29]*Ibid.,* 1.

[30]*Ibid.*

[31]"Continental Says It Will Stop Corrective Ads," *Advertising Age,* May 22, 1972, 4, 22.

[32]"$100,000,000 Class Suit Hits ITT on Profile Bread," *Advertising Age,* October 11, 1971, 3, 82.

[33]"U.S. Intensifies Barrage against Ad Field," *Advertising Age,* March 22, 1971, 1. See also "FTC Winds Up Wonder Bread, Hostess Case," *Advertising Age,* July 10, 1972, 68.

[34]"Yale Child Center Man Charges that Wonder Ad Has 'Cumulative Effect,'" *Advertising Age,* June 19, 1972, 2.

[35]*Ibid.,* 118.

[36]"FTC Staff Appeal Seeks Corrective Advertising," *Advertising Age,* April 23, 1973, 144.

[37]"Where Will It End?" *Advertising Age,* May 31, 1971, 10.

[38]Stanley E. Cohen, "Ads a 'Weak Signal' in Most Buying Decisions: Howard," *Advertising Age,* June 12, 1972, 3. See also Stephen A. Greyser, "Advertising: Attacks and Counters," *Harvard Business Review* 50 (March 1972), 22–28, 140–146 and Yale Brozen, "Advertising, the Consumer, and Inflation," *Vital Speeches,* April 1, 1972, 356–360. For assessments of the entire corrective program see John A. Howard and James Hulbert, *Advertising and the Public Interest: A Staff Report to the Federal Trade Commission,* Foreword by Robert Pitof-

sky (Chicago: Crain Communications, 1973) and William L. Wilkie, Dennis L. McNeill, and Michael B. Mazis, "Marketing's 'Scarlet Letter'" The Theory and Practice of Corrective Advertising," *Journal of Marketing* 48 (Spring 1984), 11–31.

MEANINGS

[1] Neil Postman, *Amusing Ourselves to Death: Public Discourse in the Age of Show Business* (New York: Viking, 1984), 128.

[2] Reinhold Niebuhr, *The Irony of American History* (New York: Scribners, 1952), 7.

[3] Daniel J. Boorstin, *The Image: A Guide to Pseudo-Events in America* (New York: Atheneum, 1985), 3, 5.

[4] *Ibid.*, 205.

[5] *Ibid.*, 212.

[6] Kenneth Keniston, *The Uncommitted: Alienated Youth in America* (New York: Dell, 1983), 209, 203, 229, 235.

[7] Robert Jay Lifton, "Protean Man," *Partisan Review* 35 (Winter 1968), 17.

[8] Christopher Lasch, *The Minimal Self: Psychic Survival in Troubled Times* (New York: Norton, 1984), 32.

[9] *Ibid.*, 193.

[10] Fred A. Bloom, "Psychotherapy and Moral Culture, A Psychiatrist's Field Report," *Yale Review* 66 (March 1977), 329.

[11] Fred Bloom and Alice Bloom, "Psychiatric Help 5¢: Psychoanalysis and the Psychotherapies of Liberation," *Yale Review* 68 (Spring 1979), 352.

[12] Daniel Yankelovich, *New Rules: Searching for Self-Fulfillment in a World Turned Upside Down* (New York: Random House, 1981), 246, 242.

EPILOGUE

[1] William Meyers, *The Image Makers: Power and Persuasion on Madison Avenue* (New York: Times Books, 1984), 3

[2] *Ibid.*, 9.

[3] *Ibid.*

[4] *Ibid.*, 83.

[5] *Ibid.*, 103.

[6] *Ibid.*, 126.

[7]*Ibid.,* 130, 147.
[8]*Ibid.,* 222.
[9]*Ibid,* 10.

INDEX

S

T

U

V

W